Prayertimes
with
Mother
Teresa

PRAYERTIMES
with MOTHER TERESA

◆

*A New Adventure in Prayer
Involving Scripture,
Mother Teresa, and You*

◆

Prepared by
Eileen Egan
Kathleen Egan, O.S.B.

IMAGE BOOKS
DOUBLEDAY
NEW YORK LONDON TORONTO SYDNEY AUCKLAND

AN IMAGE BOOK
PUBLISHED BY DOUBLEDAY
a division of Bantam Doubleday Dell Publishing Group, Inc.
1540 Broadway, New York, New York 10036

IMAGE, DOUBLEDAY, and the portrayal of a deer drinking
from a stream are trademarks of Doubleday, a division of
Bantam Doubleday Dell Publishing Group, Inc.

Scriptural citations are from *The New Jerusalem Bible*,
copyright © 1985 by Darton, Longman & Todd, Ltd., and Doubleday.
Used by permission of the publisher.

Excerpts from *Words to Love By . . .* by Mother Teresa, copyright © 1983
by Ave Maria Press, Notre Dame, Ind. 46556. All rights reserved.
Used with permission of the publisher.

Excerpt from *My Life for the Poor* by Mother Teresa, copyright © 1985
by José Luis Gonzalez-Balado and Janet N. Playfoot; excerpt from *Something
Beautiful for God* by Malcolm Muggeridge, copyright © 1971 by The Mother
Teresa Committee; excerpt from *Life in the Spirit* by Kathryn Spink,
copyright © 1983 by Kathryn Spink. Reprinted by permission of
Harper & Row, Publishers, Inc.

Library of Congress Cataloging-in-Publication Data
Egan, Eileen.
  Prayertimes with Mother Teresa: a new adventure in prayer
  involving Scripture, Mother Teresa, and you / Eileen Egan,
  Kathleen Egan.
    p. cm.
  Bibliography: p.
  1. Meditations. 2. Prayers. 3. Bible—Devotional literature.
4. Teresa, Mother, 1910–   . I. Egan, Kathleen. II. Title.
BX2182.2.E35 1989   89-1073
242′.2—dc19   CIP
ISBN 0-385-26231-0

This invitation to prayer
is dedicated to the memory of
Brother John Mark Egan, CFC
of Iona College, New Rochelle, New York.
His field was pastoral counseling;
his profession was love expressed
through the spiritual works of mercy.

Contents

Introductory Reflection

◆

INTERVIEWER: Mother Teresa, you love people whom oth-
                ers regard as human debris. What is your
                answer?

MOTHER TERESA: My secret is simple. I pray.

In the year marking the one thousandth anniversary of the
introduction of Christianity into Russia, the Millennium, a small
woman of seventy-eight years, bent with age, received an invitation to carry out a function unprecedented in the history of the
Soviet Union since its Revolution. Mother Teresa was asked to
bring a team of the Missionaries of Charity to carry out a charitable work.

The Soviet Union had eliminated programs of private charity, and in particular, programs under religious auspices. The
needs of citizens were in theory to be met by various state-run
organizations. Yet the formal invitation had reached her, and on
December 15, 1988, Mother Teresa, accompanied by Sister Mala,
the Indian Sister who was to be Superior of the team, were in
Moscow to prepare for the coming work among children with
various disabilities.

Before leaving for the Soviet capital, Mother Teresa talked with me about the new venture.

"The invitation was signed December eighth," she said. "We will sign a contract, and then I can bring in the other Sisters. They are in Rome, and they have been studying Russian. The Soviet authorities sent them grammar books some time ago. Someone at the Soviet Consulate helped them to practice the language.

"They are all Indian Sisters. There is good friendship between the Indian and the Russian peoples. One of the Sisters had been in Poland. Speaking Polish will make it easier for her."

Just a week earlier, on December 7, 1988, a devastating earthquake had torn up the earth in Soviet Armenia, killing tens of thousands outright and burying others under mountains of debris.

"I will go to the earthquake place, Armenia," Mother Teresa said. "Maybe we can help there as well as in Moscow. Then we would need more Sisters."

Instead of opening one house in the Soviet Union, Mother Teresa opened two, the house in Moscow on December 22, and a house in Soviet Armenia on December 26. The Sisters would plunge into work with children who had been dug out of the ruins, who had lost parents and family, and who were facing life with crushed spirits and limbs and injured bodies.

Before leaving for Moscow, Mother Teresa had taken a team of Sisters to work in a black township near Capetown, South Africa. She was encouraged by the reception she had received from forcibly relocated people as she walked among rows of squalid shacks.

"The people have suffered so much there," she said. "They were so happy when I brought them the Sisters—one black Sister from Kenya, two Sisters from India, and two white Sisters, all mixed together."

Our bloodstained century has been marked by almost inexhaustible mercilessness. A second World War destroyed cities along with their inhabitants; an unspeakable holocaust was unleashed against a people; violent revolutions and mass displacements of people left refugees by the million in Europe, Asia, the

Middle East, Africa, and mid-America. Against this background, Mother Teresa became the embodiment of inexhaustible compassion. She incarnated mercy across all barriers of race, color, and creed, and even beyond the boundaries of politics, ideologies, and nations. Already the Missionaries of Charity were working in East Germany, Poland, and Yugoslavia. The houses in the Soviet Union brought the number of centers run by the Sisters to 401 in 80 countries of the globe. Among the Sisters were women from all continents.

Even governments were disarmed by the purity of Mother Teresa's approach to human beings and their needs. When, at the invitation of a bishop, she went to Cuba, she talked with Cuba's Premier, Fidel Castro. She raised the subject of the needs of the poor. The Premier explained that the state had been organized to give the people what they needed.

"It cannot give love," commented Mother Teresa, gently pinpointing with utter exactitude what even the best-run state was unable to supply. It was not long before a team of the Missionaries of Charity was in Havana caring for the terminally ill poor. Only in Beijing was her offer of a work of mercy turned down.

The invitation to Moscow arose out of the showing of the documentary film *Mother Teresa* at the International Film Festival held in Moscow in 1987. Ann and Jeanette Petrie, producers of the film, reported that many in the audience were visibly moved to tears and expressed their appreciation of it by an ovation. The film won the Soviet Peace Committee Prize, and later Mother Teresa herself received the highest award of the Soviet Peace Committee, a Gold Medal. She accepted it in the name of the world's poor.

CALCUTTA

Some forty years earlier, Mother Teresa had stepped out alone on the streets of a scourged city, Calcutta, capital of a scourged province, Bengal. She found homeless refugees dying at her feet. She was a woman of prayer before she encountered the boundless misery caused by the descent of four million destitute refugees from across a nearby border. Until her eighteenth year, she lived in a devout family in Skopje, Yugoslavia, a meeting place of varied cultures and religious traditions. For twenty years she had lived a deep prayer life as a religious Sister.

When Mother Teresa picked up the first dying woman from a Calcutta street, a barely recognizable scrap of humanity soiled by dirt and spittle, she did not know that this rescue would be the first of thousands upon thousands. In coming decades an unending line of desolate human beings would need to be saved from dying like animals in the gutter. Nor could she have dreamed that her name would become so inextricably bound with the agonies of Calcutta that the name of the city would be affixed to her own name.

Had that compassion been grounded in human sympathy alone, could it have survived the next forty years of serving the poorest of the poor wherever they could be found? Could that compassion have proved inexhaustible without the undergirding of prayer? Mother Teresa asserts that it could not.

"There is no one," she asserts, "who needs God's grace and help more than I do. I think that is why He uses me, because I cannot claim any credit for what gets done."

Not only does she see herself as simply a channel through which the Good News of God's love can flow, but in each suffering person she sees the clear vision of God's image.

KALIGHAT

Of all the works of Mother Teresa and the Missionaries of Charity, the one that expressed most dramatically her vision of the person, her wonder at the glory of each person as a shining-forth of the divine spirit, was Kalighat, the Home for the Dying in

Calcutta. It was the one that eventually drew most attention to her work.

Some of those near death had been cared for by Mother Teresa in dirt-floored rooms in the Moti Jihl slum. Others were brought, by taxi when rupees were available and taxi drivers willing, to local hospitals. When a jam-packed hospital refused one of her helpless charges, Mother Teresa would stand her ground, waiting by the side of the suffering person until a corner could be found. In time, the City Fathers of Calcutta gave Mother Teresa a place to bring the destitute dying. It was the hostel formerly used by the poorest pilgrims to the shrine of the goddess Kali, the goddess of destruction and purification. Nearby was the cremation place, the ghat, hence the name Kalighat.

It was a busy place, since a constant stream of pilgrims came to the shrine where the image of Kali, dark-visaged and garlanded with the necklace of skulls, stood poised in her immemorial dance. Residents of Calcutta and its many visitors were assailed by hungry beggars, by the young and the aged, by mothers with scrawny infants, and were appalled by the army of the shelterless who lay down to sleep on dirty sidewalks. They learned of a place where those who lacked everything received free from the Missionaries of Charity what others could only get for money.

Instead of a place of horror and despair, those of us familiar with Kalighat found a place of peacefulness where the gratitude of those who had been abandoned by all was palpable. So also was the gratitude—and even spiritual joy—of Mother Teresa and the Sisters. Their joy came from serving those whom they saw as Jesus in a distressing disguise, and nurturing life itself, the greatest gift of God. It became easy to see everyone before us bathed in the light of the incarnation.

Some of those brought to Kalighat seemed so forsaken that nothing could rouse them, but we saw how Mother Teresa and the Sisters succeeded in consoling the almost inconsolable. It was not long before volunteers from all walks of life, religions, and castes came to help in Kalighat.

The spirit of the Sisters was expressed in the constitution. "Our homes for the dying are treasure houses for the opportunities they afford us to reach souls. Death sacred to all men–is the final stage of complete development on this earth. Having lived well, we wish for ourselves and for all men to die beautifully and so enter into the eternal life of full development in God. We train ourselves to be extremely kind and gentle in touch of hand, tone of voice, and in our smile so as to make the Mercy of God very real and to induce the dying person to turn to God with filial confidence."

Mother Teresa had a special impact on Christians in reminding people that God's love was always with them, and in bringing to life Christ's words, "I am with you always." No matter how they met death, they would never die alone; they would at all times be accompanied by Jesus.

Kalighat revealed to those who had known the ultimate in rejection that merciful love existed in the world. Mother Teresa offered a proof to those deprived of all, of dignity and the respect of others, that they were possessed of infinite dignity as children of God. She made the discovery that whatever their tradition, people did not object to being treated as one would treat the Savior.

It was her unremitting work to validate the inviolable dignity of each person, in particular the work at Kalighat, that brought Mother Teresa the highest accolade, the Nobel Peace Prize. Robert S. McNamara, head of the World Bank and a prominent Presbyterian layman, in nominating her for the Nobel award, stated that she deserved it "because she promotes peace in the most fundamental manner by her confirmation of the inviolability of human dignity."

OSLO

When Mother Teresa accepted the Nobel Peace Prize at Oslo, Norway, the anthem of praise was a harmonious one. Oslo gave her a platform to communicate in words the message of her life and work. It did not occur to her to temper her message. Someone has said, "Her language is the language of her being, the voice of the Christian's Good News, as mysteriously and essentially hers as is the unmistakable grain pattern of an oak its individual signature."

"It hurt Jesus to love us," she told the Nobel award gathering and the world press. "It hurt Him. And to make sure we remember His great love, He made himself the bread of life to satisfy our hunger for His love—our hunger for God—because we have been created for that love. We have been created in His image. We have been created to love and be loved, and He has become man to make it possible for us to love as He loved us. He makes himself the hungry one, the naked one, the homeless one, the sick one, the one in prison, the lonely one, the unwanted one, and He says, 'You did it to Me!' "

Mother Teresa was putting into concrete terms the new relationship that should mark those who chose to be followers of Jesus. It was the merciful relationship announced in the great parable of the Last Judgment when Jesus identified Himself for all time with the least of humankind. Mother Teresa seemed to incarnate the Beatitude, "Blessed are the merciful, they shall have mercy shown them."

What brought joy to Mother Teresa was the fact that at Oslo the works of mercy—feeding the hungry, clothing the naked, sheltering the shelterless—were being recognized as works of peace. A few contrary voices were later raised on this point. The objection was that Mother Teresa addressed the needs of the individual and failed to confront the structures that cause the poverty that gives rise to strife and violence. She felt that this was another vocation, but never budged from the conviction that love and care for the individual must undergird any work for human betterment.

"If there are people who feel God wants them to change the structures of society," she said, "that is something between them and God. We must serve Him in whatever way we are called. I am called to help the individual, to love each poor person, not to deal with institutions." She did not demean other vocations, since institutions certainly needed changing. Her revolution was a revolution of love, of living to the fullest the new relationship taught by Jesus. This relationship was supposed to be carried into society by the "new creature" of the gospel. Can any revolution improve the lot of the poor and oppressed if mercy is set aside?

Mother Teresa's defense of life is well-known, in particular her defense of the life of the unborn against abortion; less well-known is her defense of the human family against preparations for war. "The presence of the nuclear bomb in the world," she says, "has created fear and distrust among nations, as it is one more weapon to destroy human life—God's beautiful presence in the world."

A special gift of Mother Teresa is her power to be a point of reconciliation between vastly different and even antagonistic persons and groups. They may have nothing in common with each other, and may be mutually incompatible, but they unite in recognizing Mother Teresa as a person to be emulated. The Communist Chief Minister of Bengal held a reception in Mother Teresa's honor when she returned from the Nobel award ceremonies. "You have been the Mother of Bengal," he stated, "and now you are the Mother of the world."

When a group of people, belonging to a multiplicity of traditions and led by a follower of Gandhi, promoted a Prayer for Peace to be recited around the world, they decided it should have a public launching. They came to the conviction that the event could have full meaning only "if the prayer were given the authority of someone of manifest purity of heart, someone whose life was a way of peace. . . . It was felt that the appropriate person would live in the most common thoroughfare of the world, that of the poor, and would demonstrably see in the face of various teeming humanity the single countenance of the Son of Peace."

Their decision was to call on Mother Teresa to launch the prayer.

As her first prescription for peace is prayer, Mother Teresa accepted, and recited publicly in London, "Lead me from Death to Life, from Falsehood to Truth. Lead me from Despair to Hope, from Fear to Trust. Lead me from Hate to Love, from War to Peace. Let Peace be in our Heart, our World, our Universe. Peace. Peace. Peace."

Mother Teresa commended the Peace Prayer to her lay Co-Workers around the world. Over the years, as the Missionaries of Charity, Sisters and Brothers, and at length, priests, were growing in number, so were the lay Co-Workers. Their life was also fed by springs of prayer; for the Christians among them, the daily prayers included the Peace Prayer attributed to St. Francis, the prayer of Cardinal Newman, and the prayer of Pope Paul VI (all included in "A Retreat in the Spirit of Mother Teresa and the Missionaries of Charity," page 121).

"Love to pray," Mother Teresa told the Co-Workers. "Feel often during the day the need for prayer, and take trouble to pray. Prayer enlarges the heart until it is capable of containing God's gift of Himself. Ask and seek and your heart will grow big enough to receive Him."

The Co-Workers pay no dues, but pray together as often as possible. Jointly or singly, they try to do "something beautiful for God" by meeting the needs of others. These needs may be of the spirit—especially in the developed world—as well as the needs of the body. They always have the example of Mother Teresa in the strength to stand alone, if necessary, and with love, to speak up against what is against human life and human dignity. Persons of any tradition may join the Co-Workers as long as they share the vision of Mother Teresa. They find strength in "being part of a worldwide company of those who bear witness to the presence of God in every member of the family of man." She talked to the Co-Workers in the West of the need to share what they had in surplus and to be constantly aware of the danger of being suffocated by possessions and by the breathless pace of life.

Bengal, with its famine, its violence, and its masses of refugees, had presented to Mother Teresa a microcosm of the world at large. It called for an unprecedented outpouring of the works of mercy, and she responded. The world today is enduring similar but unspeakably greater scourges and calls for a greater concentration on the works of mercy than has been known until now. Yet governments put vastly more of their resources into works of war than into works of mercy for the famine-stricken, for victims of violence in many quarters, and into sheltering and finding homes for refugees. If the war that is being prepared at a ruinous cost to the world's people were to occur, every work of mercy would be reversed. This would put humanity itself in peril.

Mercy, Mother Teresa reminds us, is only love under the aspect of need, love in action that can serve as the undergirding of peace. On occasion she gives a message in five words. She raises her gnarled, work-worn hands, hands that have helped those in agony to endure the unendurable, and points with her right forefinger to each of the fingers of her left hand. "You did it to Me."

Using Prayertimes

♦

The stories told by Mother Teresa are like little parables, parables of everyday life about ordinary people, particularly the poor. Even at the Nobel Peace Prize ceremonies, her acceptance speech was studded with parables, all related to the teaching of Jesus, above all, to the great parable of the Last Judgment.

The stories of Mother Teresa's doings recounted by others often share the same parable-like quality. "Living the Word" comprises both her own stories and those told about her work.

Those of us who have been present at Mother Teresa's talks and interviews over the years know that she tells each story as if it had happened the day before. The event, so vivid to her, becomes alive to her hearers, her words taking fire from the witness of her life.

For each of the fifty-two weeks of the year, something fresh awaits the reader.

Prayertimes links the story-parables with Mother Teresa's spiritual reflections, and joins both with a passage from Scripture. It is hoped that the first-of-a-kind offering may enliven prayer life for people of any age group, especially hard-pressed, busy people caught up in a round of numberless duties and worries. It may appeal to teenagers who find themselves turned off by more conventional approaches to prayer.

It would not be surprising for a reader, coming on *Prayertimes* for the first time, to race through it. A radically different approach is suggested after a possible cursory reading. Taking the facing pages of "Week One," for example, the reader is asked to spend at least fifteen minutes pondering them. This may sound simpler than it actually is.

To spend fifteen minutes on the same passages every day for a week may be a bit difficult for those not accustomed or not able to find time for meditation. From one moment to the next, a light may shine from "The Word," from "Words of Mother Teresa," or from how our lives are relating to "Living the Word." New and unexpected insights may spring up in the heart, the mind, and the imagination.

A short prayer to the Sanctifying Spirit and the Lord's Prayer might be the most fruitful way to lead into *Prayertimes*. Fr. Basil Pennington, in his book, *Centering Prayer*, gives wise counsel: "I would like to encourage you to stop for a bit and turn to the Holy Spirit, dwelling within you. He is your Spirit, the Gift given to you at baptism to be your very own spirit."

"No one was ever so conscious that he was a son of God," wrote an unbeliever, Ernest Renan, concerning St. Francis of Assisi. The same could be said regarding Mother Teresa. It is as a child of a loving God that she can live out her days in total trust, in total surrender. She invites everyone she meets to share that same trust, that same surrender.

When we recite the Lord's Prayer, we might place ourselves in the crowd that surrounded Jesus on the mountain that day. They heard the Beatitudes:

How blessed are the poor in spirit:
the kingdom of heaven is theirs.
Blessed are the merciful:
they shall have mercy shown them.

Then they heard for the first time,

You should pray like this:
Our Father in heaven,
May your name be held holy,
your kingdom come . . .

We can take guidance from what St. Cyprian of Carthage, the first African bishop-martyr, wrote on the Lord's Prayer about 250 A.D.

In reminding us that Jesus did not teach us to say, "My Father," Cyprian added, "The teacher of Peace and Master of Unity did not want prayer to be something individualistic and self-centered. He who inculcated oneness wanted each one to pray for all, just as He Himself bore all in One." We are warned not to make prayer a showy display, but even when we pray in secret, we are praying to the Father of all as members of the people of God. In that sense, even when we pray alone, our prayer is communal.

Some points on using *Prayertimes:*

1. To find spiritual nourishment in "The Word," "Living the Word," and "Words of Mother Teresa," it is necessary to find a place where as far as possible one can escape noise and avoid interruptions. Even speed readers must slow down and read each sentence with relaxed slowness.

2. A first necessity is mindfulness, the harnessing of scattered thoughts—a never-ending struggle. Each distraction, each worry, each disappointment, each angry thought can be placed at the feet of Jesus. In "Week One" we learn that the crowds placed at the feet of the Lord their lame, crippled, blind, and dumb, and he cured them (Matthew 15:29-31). The crowds were moved to praise God. We can also praise God for His gifts to us, even for His greatest gift, the gift that we are alive and able to sing his praises.

3. Especially after pondering the scriptural "Word," we may become still and wait on the Lord. What is His word to our waiting spiritual ear? From the earliest days of the church, "divine reading" was practiced as a way to reach God. We may memorize the passage from Scripture, or parts of it, or take time to read its Biblical setting. A few

words of Scripture learned by heart may spring into the mind when they are most needed to console or inspire.

4.   The "Response" to *Prayertimes* may at first be passive. We are accustomed to saying our prayers and moving on to other things. A response may not come immediately. When it comes, it may be no more than a word, but it is *your word*. This might lead into a form of "centering" prayer described by Fr. Basil Pennington in his book. We search for a word, a phrase, our own cry to God, that can unlock the love in a tired and tepid heart. It might be "Lamb of God," reminding us how tender, gentle, and helpless is the Lamb that allowed Himself to die on the Cross for us. Other words might be "mercy," "forgiving," "reconciling." Let your word take root in your heart from constant repetition.

As you become more and more adept at removing yourself for a time from the demands of a world clamoring for attention, you may find a prayer rising from the depths of your spirit. It may be a prayer of thanks for a special gift or insight, or a prayer to rid your heart of bitterness that still rankles from an old slight or insult. You might pray to find the right words to praise someone seldom praised or to give recognition to someone usually taken for granted.

You may pull from your memory a parable of your own life or the life of your family. It may be a simple event or comment that served to awaken a new sympathy or to give your life a new direction. The resulting action might include joining a group working for justice, peace, and hope for the deprived.

The compilers of *Prayertimes* had a mother always at the ready with a moral lesson from everyday events. Any slighting words from us about a schoolgirl with badly crossed eyes, or a schoolboy slow to learn but quick to arouse ridicule in class and community with ludicrous antics, was met with an assertion.

"Thank God for His goodness to you," she would tell us. "Remember always, 'There but for the grace of God go I.' " An expansion of sympathy, even an identification with the impaired and wounded, entered our lives during grammar school days.

Prayertimes may help lead the reader to a closer relationship with God. Your "Responses" written on these pages may describe something of the growth of that relationship or some aspect of transformation, and may become a record of your own faith journey.

Besides the parables she relates to her Sisters, to Co-Workers, and to audiences from the Australian outback to Las Vegas, Nevada, Mother Teresa lets fall from her lips golden nuggets. These have made a deep impression on countless people.

"God has not called us to be successful," she states. "He has called us to be faithful."

For those striving to deepen their life of prayer, it is a matter of being faithful to the quest, confident that God will do the rest.

We all do not have the same capacity, the same intensity, the same insights. We can take to heart the words of the Litany of Humility recited by the Missionaries of Charity. "That others may become holier than I, provided that I may become as holy as I should, Jesus grant me the grace to desire it."

The Weeks

♦

WEEK ONE

The Word

Matthew 15: 29–31

Jesus went on from there and reached the shores of the Lake of Galilee, and he went up onto the mountain. He took his seat, and large crowds came to him bringing the lame, the crippled, the blind, the dumb and many others; these they put down at his feet, and he cured them. The crowds were astonished to see the dumb speaking, the cripples whole again, the lame walking, and the blind with their sight, and they praised the God of Israel.

Living the Word

The first woman I saw I myself picked up from the street. She had been half eaten by the rats and ants. I took her to the hospital, but they could not do anything for her. They only took her in because I refused to move until they accepted her. From there I went to the municipality, and I asked them to give me a place where I could bring these people because on the same day I had found other people dying in the streets. The health officer of the municipality took me to the temple, the Kali Temple, and showed me the *darmashalah* where the people used to rest after they had done their worship of Kali goddess. It was an empty building; he asked me if I would accept it. I was very happy to have that place for many reasons, but especially knowing that it was a center of worship and devotion of the Hindus. *SBFG 91*

Words of Mother Teresa

A Second Calling

In 1946 I was going to Darjeeling to make my retreat. It was on that train I heard the call to give up all and follow Him into the slums, to serve Him among the poorest of the poor.

I knew it was His will and that I had to follow Him. There was no doubt that it was going to be His work.

It was a call within my vocation. It was a second calling. It was a vocation to give up even Loreto, where I was very happy, to go out in the streets to serve the poorest of the poor.

SBFG 85, 86

My Words

A prayer, a modified attitude,
A new sympathy, an action?

_____

_____

_____

_____

_____

_____

_____

_____

_____

_____

WEEK TWO

The Word

Proverbs 16:19–20

> Better be humble with the poor
>   than share the booty with the proud.

> Whoever listens closely to the word finds happiness;
>   whoever trusts Yahweh is blessed.

Living the Word

In December Mother Teresa decided to start her work in one of Calcutta's most desolate slums. She gathered a few children around her and started an open-air school. She began it "right on the ground," drawing the letters of the alphabet with a stick in the dusty earth.

When it came time to take her midday meal, she would look for a quiet place where she could find drinking water. Once, she knocked at the door of a convent to ask if she could come inside to take her meal. She was told to go around to the back and was left to eat her sparse food under the back stairs like a street beggar. "God wants me to be a lonely nun," she wrote, "laden with the poverty of the Cross. Today I learned a good lesson. The poverty of the poor is so hard."   *SAV 43*

Words of Mother Teresa

LET JESUS USE US WITHOUT CONSULTING US

On many occasions Mother Teresa was the recipient of the key to this or that city, once receiving the key to New York City from the hands of Mayor Koch. The ritual was one that was strange to her. Once, after she had been told that she was the first citizen of a midwestern town, she spoke with a group of Co-Workers.

"Yesterday," she said, "I was the first citizen, and I said, 'Thank you very much.' But I don't understand what it means. It makes no difference; it is coming from the same hand. And tomorrow, if people would say 'Crucify'—all right. It is the same loving hand. That acceptance for you and for me—it is what Jesus wants from us. To allow Him to use us without consulting us."

SAV 418

My Words

> *A prayer, a modified attitude,*
> *A new sympathy, an action?*

_____

_____

_____

_____

_____

_____

_____

WEEK THREE

The Word

Letter of Paul to the Philippians 4:4–7

Always be joyful, then, in the Lord: I repeat, be joyful. Let your good sense be obvious to everybody. The Lord is near. Never worry about anything; but tell God all your desires of every kind in prayer and petition shot through with gratitude, and the peace of God which is beyond our understanding will guard your hearts and your thoughts in Christ Jesus.

Living the Word

We do God's work. He provides the means.

If He does not give us the means, that shows that He does not want the work. So why worry?

One day Mr. Thomas, the chairman of Hindustan Lever, came to offer a property in Bombay.

He first asked me, "Mother, how is your work financed?"

I answered him, "Mr. Thomas, who sent you here?"

"I felt an urge inside me," he said.

"Well, other people like you come to see me and say the same. That is my budget," I said.

I hope you are not giving only your surplus. You must give what costs you, make a sacrifice, go without something you like, that your gift may have value before God. Then you will be truly brothers and sisters to the poor who are deprived of even the things they need. *MLFP 32*

Words of Mother Teresa

ASK AND BELIEVE

Our dependence on Divine Providence is a firm and lively faith that God can and will help us. That He can is evident, because He is almighty; that He will is certain because He promised it in so many passages of Holy Scripture and because He is infinitely faithful to all His promises. Christ encourages us to have this confidence in these words: "Whatever you ask in prayer, believe that you have received it, and it will be yours." The apostle St. Peter also commands us to throw all cares upon the Lord who provides for us. And why should God not care for us since He sent us His Son and with Him all? *LIS 27*

My Words

A prayer, a modified attitude,
A new sympathy, an action?

_____

_____

_____

_____

_____

_____

_____

_____

_____

_____

WEEK FOUR

The Word

Matthew 25:31–36

> When the Son of man comes in his glory, escorted by all the
> angels, then he will take his seat on his throne of glory. All
> nations will be assembled before him and he will separate
> people one from another as the shepherd separates sheep
> from goats. He will place the sheep on his right hand and the
> goats on his left. Then the King will say to those on his right
> hand, "Come, you whom my Father has blessed, take as your
> heritage the kingdom prepared for you since the foundation
> of the world. For I was hungry and you gave me food. I was
> thirsty and you gave me drink. I was a stranger and you made
> me welcome, lacking clothes and you clothed me, sick and
> you visited me, in prison and you came to see me."

Living the Word

It was in 1955 that Mother Teresa took me through Kalighat,
the Home for the Dying. In the men's ward she told me what she
knew of each one. She went from pallet to pallet, talking with and
consoling men and women from whom life had taken everything
but breath itself.

The pilgrims' hostel, or *darmashalah,* was constructed like an
ancient inn. In the middle of the long hall was a wide passageway.
The pallets were arranged at right angles along the sides and
were raised about two feet from the floor. Lying side by side on
the cement raised platforms were seventy men of all ages. Mother
Teresa recalled the words of a man at Kalighat, "I have lived like
an animal on the street, but I die like an angel."   *SAV 56*

Words of Mother Teresa

Jesus in His Distressing Disguise

Looking about at the rows of human beings stretched on pallets in the hostel, Mother Teresa said, "Our work calls for us to see Jesus in everyone. He has told us that He is the hungry one. He is the naked one. He is the thirsty one. He is the one without a home. He is the one who is suffering. These are our treasures.

"They are Jesus. Each one is Jesus in His distressing disguise." "Jesus in His distressing disguise." It was that phrase that rang in my brain. Jesus, covered with spittle, in the gutter, Jesus assaulted by maggots, Jesus crying out for being forsaken.   *SAV 57*

My Words

A prayer, a modified attitude,
A new sympathy, an action?

_____

_____

_____

_____

_____

_____

_____

_____

_____

_____

WEEK FIVE

The Word

Letter of James 2:5–6, 8–9

> It was those who were poor according to the world that God chose, to be rich in faith and to be the heirs to the kingdom which he promised to those who love him. You, on the other hand, have dishonoured the poor. Is it not the rich who lord it over you?
>
> Well, the right thing to do is to keep the supreme Law of scripture: *you will love your neighbour as yourself;* but as soon as you make class distinctions, you are committing sin and under condemnation for breaking the Law.

Living the Word

The fifteenth slum school was opened in a corner of Calcutta inhabited by a cluster of lepers.

The parents, I found out, began to argue among themselves, some saying that the Sisters would carry the children away to a hospital. The Muslims approached the Sisters to find out if they were going to make their children Christian.

It took about a week for the wary observers to believe that the Sisters were doing exactly what they had promised, giving their children a free elementary school education.

Mother Teresa visited the school and talked in a low tone to Sister Angela. "This boy has white spots on his face. Be sure, Sister, that he comes to the clinic. That little girl in the first row, too." I felt as though a sentence were being passed over each little head, a sentence to one of the most dread diseases ever to afflict humankind. *SAV 68–69*

Words of Mother Teresa

STREETS OF CALCUTTA TO EVERYONE'S DOOR

"The Streets of Calcutta lead to everyone's door, and the very pain, the very ruin of our Calcutta is the heart's witness to the glory that once was. I know you think you should make a trip to Calcutta, but I strongly advise you to save your airfare and spend it on the poor in your own country.

"It is easy to love the people far away. It is not always easy to love those who live right next to us. There are thousands of people dying for a piece of bread. There are thousands more dying for a little bit of love, for a little bit of acknowledgment.

"This is one station of the Cross; Jesus present in those who are hungry and falling under the weight of the Cross.

"Today, in the world, is an 'open Calvary.' People throughout the world may look different or have a different religion, education, or position, but they are all the same. They are people to be loved. They are all hungry for love." *CoW-N*

My Words

> *A prayer, a modified attitude,*
> *A new sympathy, an action?*

_____

_____

_____

_____

_____

_____

WEEK SIX

The Word

Isaiah 44:1–3

And now listen, Jacob my servant,
Israel whom I have chosen.
Thus says Yahweh who made you,
who formed you in the womb; he will help you.
Do not be afraid, Jacob my servant,
Jeshurun whom I have chosen.
For I shall pour out water on the thirsty soil
and streams on the dry ground.
I shall pour out my spirit on your descendants,
my blessing on your offspring.

Living the Word

A young Brother came to Mother Teresa seeking advice. He wanted only one assignment, to work with the lepers. Mother told him that his vocation was not necessarily to work with the lepers. His vocation was to belong to Jesus, and because he belonged to Jesus, he could put his love for Jesus in action by service to the lepers.

"It makes no difference whether you are teaching university-level people, or whether you are in the slums, or just cleaning or washing or scrubbing, washing wounds, picking up maggots, all this makes no difference. Not what we do, but how much love we put into doing is what concerns Jesus." *MDV 25*

Words of Mother Teresa

A PRAYER OF MOTHER TERESA

Eternal life, Father, is to know You, the one true God, and Jesus Christ, whom You have sent.

May we bring this eternal life to the poor, deprived as they are of all comfort, of material possessions; may they come to know You, love You, possess You, share in Your life, You who are the God and Father of men and of my Lord Jesus Christ, Source of all truth and goodness and happiness.   *WDI 34*

My Words

A prayer, a modified attitude,
A new sympathy, an action?

_____

_____

_____

_____

_____

_____

_____

_____

_____

_____

_____

WEEK SEVEN

The Word

First Letter of Peter 2:21–24

This, in fact, is what you were called to do, because Christ suffered for you and left an example for you to follow in his steps. He had done nothing wrong, and *had spoken no deceit.* He was insulted and did not retaliate with insults; when he was suffering he made no threats but put his trust in the upright judge. He was *bearing our sins* in his own body on the cross, so that we might die to our sins and live for uprightness; *through his bruises you have been healed.*

Living the Word

Among our lepers there are many well-educated people, many rich and capable people. But owing to the disease, they have been thrown out of society, out of their homes, by their relations, and very often even their own children do not want to see them anymore. They get isolated from their own families and have no alternative but to turn to begging. Very often you see people coming up to Bengal from the south and the Bengal people going to the farthest north just to be far away from the people and from the places where they have been known and served and loved. We have among our lepers here in Calcutta very capable people who have had very high positions in life. But owing to the disease, they are now living in the slums, unknown, unloved, and uncared for. Thank God our Sisters are there to love them and to be their friends.   *SBFG 102*

Words of Mother Teresa

"IN OUR PEOPLE—CALVARY"

At Christmas I was talking to our lepers
and telling them that the leprosy is a gift from God,
that God can trust them so much
that He gives them this terrible suffering. . . .

And one man
who was completely disfigured
started pulling at my sari.
   "Repeat that," he said.
   "Repeat that this is God's love.
   Those who are suffering understand you when you
      talk like this, Mother Teresa."

Christ is really living his passion in these homes.
In our people you can see Calvary.   *WTLB 65*

My Words

A prayer, a modified attitude,
A new sympathy, an action?

_____
_____
_____
_____
_____
_____

WEEK EIGHT

The Word

Second Letter of Paul to the Corinthians 9:6–11

Remember: anyone who sows sparsely will reap sparsely as well–and anyone who sows generously will reap generously as well. Each one should give as much as he has decided on his own initiative, not reluctantly or under compulsion, for *God loves a cheerful giver.* God is perfectly able to enrich you with every grace, so that you always have enough for every conceivable need, and your resources overflow in all kinds of good work. As scripture says: *To the needy he gave without stint, his uprightness stands firm forever.*

The one who so freely provides *seed for the sower and food to eat* will provide you with ample store of seed for sowing and make *the harvest of your uprightness* a bigger one.

Living the Word

Mother Teresa related the story of the rich man in India who wanted to bank an immense amount of money for the Sisters, so that they would not find themselves someday without support or funds for the work.

"The condition was," Mother Teresa explained, "that this money should not be touched. It should be a security for the work. So I wrote back and said that rather than offend God, I would offend him a little bit, though I was grateful for his thoughtfulness. I could not accept the money because all these years God has taken care of us, and the security of this money would take away the very life of the work. I could not have money in the bank while people were starving.

"It shocked him," she went on, "it shook him. Before he died, he sent the money, so much for the lepers, so much for the Home for the Dying, so much for food, and so on. He gave it all."

SAV 390

Words of Mother Teresa

THE WORK OF NOW: THE WORK OF TOMORROW

"For us it's not a waste of time or life to spend that time just feeding the person today. The work of tomorrow? There are many people who can do that, who can remove the works of injustice and so on. But for us that person needs a shelter now. I think our part is fulfilled there. And by doing our part many people are getting concerned to do the second part—to improve and to help the people, to remove that poverty and that hunger and that nakedness." *TGLC 75–76*

My Words

A prayer, a modified attitude,
A new sympathy, an action?

_____

_____

_____

_____

_____

_____

_____

WEEK NINE

The Word

Letter of Paul to the Philippians 4:8–9

Let your minds be filled with everything that is true, everything that is honourable, everything that is upright and pure,
everything that we love and admire–with whatever is good
and praiseworthy. Keep doing everything you learnt from me
and were told by me and have heard or seen me doing. Then
the God of peace will be with you.

Living the Word

"I remember, when we first came to New York," Mother
Teresa related, "and Cardinal Cooke wanted to give every Sister
five hundred dollars every month. And I looked at him, I said,
'Cardinal, do you think God is going to be bankrupt in New
York?' He looked at me, thinking, *Maybe she's a little bit off*. He has
brought it up again, again, and again, and each time I answered
the same way.

"A Sister was coming to join the Society, and we had not
enough cotton to make a mattress for her, and I told the Sisters,
'Take my pillow, I can sleep without a pillow, and finish the
mattress.' But they refused. So I got up and I took that pillow to
them. There was a knock at the gate. The Sister ran down and
there was an Englishman with a big cotton mattress. He said, 'I'm
going to England, I thought Mother Teresa would like to have
the mattress.'"   *Talk Four*

Words of Mother Teresa

MONEY IS NOT ENOUGH

"Today, as before, when Jesus comes among His own, His own don't know Him. He comes in the rotting bodies of the poor. He comes even in the rich who are being suffocated by their riches, in the loneliness of their hearts, and there is no one to love them. Jesus comes to you and to me. And often, very often, we pass Him by. Here in England, and in many other places such as Calcutta, we find lonely people who are known only by their addresses, by the number of their room. Where are we, then? Do we really know that there are such people? . . .

"These are the people we must know. This is Jesus yesterday and today and tomorrow, and you and I must know who they are. That knowledge will lead us to love them. And that love, to service. Let us not be satisfied with just paying money. Money is not enough. Money can be got. They need your hand to serve them. They need your hearts to love them." *SAV 251*

My Words

A prayer, a modified attitude,
A new sympathy, an action?

_____

_____

_____

_____

_____

WEEK TEN

The Word

Letter of Paul to Titus 3:4–7

But when the kindness and love of God our Saviour for mankind were revealed, it was not because of any upright actions we had done ourselves; it was for no reason except his own faithful love that he saved us, by means of the cleansing water of rebirth and renewal in the Holy Spirit which he has so generously poured over us through Jesus Christ our Saviour; so that, justified by his grace, we should become heirs in hope of eternal life.

Letter of Paul to the Ephesians 3:20–21

Glory to him whose power, working in us, can do infinitely more than we can ask or imagine.

Living the Word

At the Home for the Dying that the Missionaries of Charity have in Calcutta, there was a man who had cancer, his body half-consumed by the sickness. Everyone had abandoned him as a hopeless case. Mother Teresa came near him to wash him tenderly. She encountered, at first, only the sick man's disdain.

"How can you stand my body's stench?" he asked.

Then, quite calmly, the dying man said to her, "You're not from here. The people here don't behave the way you do."

Several minutes went by. And then the terminally ill man murmured a typical Indian expression: "Glory to you, woman."

"No," replied Mother Teresa. "Glory to you who suffer with Christ."

Then they smiled at each other. The sick man's suffering seemed to stop. He died two days later. *SOMT 13*

Words of Mother Teresa

Bitterness an Infectious Disease

We must have the courage
to pray to have the courage to accept.
Because we do not pray enough, we see only the
    human part.
We don't see the divine,
And we resent it.

I think that much of the misunderstanding of suffering
        today
    comes from that,
    from resentment and bitterness.
Bitterness is an infectious disease,
    a cancer,
    an anger hidden inside. *WTLB 68*

My Words

A prayer, a modified attitude,
A new sympathy, an action?

_____
_____
_____
_____
_____
_____

WEEK ELEVEN

The Word

Letter of Paul to the Colossians 1:9–14

We have never failed to remember you in our prayers and ask that through perfect wisdom and spiritual understanding you should reach the fullest knowledge of his will and so be able to lead a life worthy of the Lord, a life acceptable to him in all its aspects, bearing fruit in every kind of good work and growing in knowledge of God, fortified, in accordance with his glorious strength, with all power always to persevere and endure, giving thanks with joy to the Father who has made you able to share the lot of God's holy people and with them to inherit the light.

Because that is what he has done. It is he who has rescued us from the ruling force of darkness and transferred us to the kingdom of the Son that he loves.

Living the Word

One of the abandoned children we had in our *Shishu Bhavan* I gave to a very high-class and rich family.

After a few months I heard that the child had become very sick and completely disabled. So I went to that family and said, "Give me back the child and I will give you a healthy child."

The father looked at me and said, "Take my life first, then take the child."

He loved the child from his heart!

In Calcutta every night we send word to all the clinics, to all the police stations, to all the hospitals, "Please do not destroy the child; we'll take the child."

So our house is always full of children. (There is a joke in Calcutta: "Mother Teresa is always talking about family planning

and about abortion, but she has certainly not practiced this at all:
every day she has more and more children.")   *MLFP 64*

Words of Mother Teresa

A LIFELONG SHARING

Love cannot remain by itself—it has no meaning.
Love has to be put into action
and that action is service.

How do we put the love for God in action?
By being faithful to our family,
   to the duties that God has entrusted to us.
Whatever form we are,
   able or disabled,
   rich or poor,
it is not how much we do
but how much love we put in the doing
   —a lifelong sharing of love with others.   *WTLB 75*

My Words

> *A prayer, a modified attitude,*
> *A new sympathy, an action?*

_____

_____

_____

_____

_____

_____

WEEK TWELVE

The Word

Luke 12:22-26

He said to his disciples, "That is why I am telling you not to worry about your life and what you are to eat, nor about your body and how you are to clothe it. For life is more than food, and the body more than clothing. Think of the ravens. They do not sow or reap; they have no storehouses and no barns; yet God feeds them. And how much more you are worth than the birds! Can any of you, however much you worry, add a single cubit to your span of life? If a very small thing is beyond your powers, why worry about the rest?"

Living the Word

When asked if she worried about the safety of the Sisters as they left, two by two, in the early mornings to go to the bustees, Mother Teresa replied that they were in the hands of the Lord. The slum areas were not only fetid but often dangerous.

"They pray their way, even on the trams. When they walk, they recite the rosary." I thought of the low voices of the young women, repeating the "Our Father" and including in "Father" all the children of the human family, all the people around them who had their own name and concept of the Creator.

"Now, they tell me," said Mother Teresa with a smile that brought a quick brightness to her eyes, "the time that it takes to reach different places by the number of rosaries they can say. 'It took us three rosaries to get there, Mother,' they tell me. When they pray as they go along, the people see it and respect them. In India there is a great respect for holiness, even among the rascals.

SAV 106

Words of Mother Teresa

POVERTY IS LOVE BEFORE IT IS RENUNCIATION

"Let us not look for substitutes which restore to us the wealth we have renounced."–*M.T.*

Christ, who being poor and emptied himself to work out our redemption, calls us:
to listen to the voice of the poor, especially in our times, which urges us to make reparation for the selfishness and greed of man, craving for earthly riches and power to the point of injustice to others.
Our poverty should be true Gospel poverty, gentle, tender, glad, and openhearted, always ready to give an expression of love. Poverty is love before it is renunciation.   *Const.*

My Words

A prayer, a modified attitude,
A new sympathy, an action?

_____

_____

_____

_____

_____

_____

_____

WEEK THIRTEEN

The Word

Matthew 5:7–8

> Blessed are the merciful:
> they shall have mercy shown them.
> Blessed are the pure in heart:
> they shall see God.

Living the Word

Mother Teresa came to Las Vegas in 1960 to address the National Council of Catholic Women. The invitation, tendered by Catholic Relief Services, brought Mother Teresa out of India for the first time since her arrival there in 1929. She thanked the Catholic women for their support of her Mother and Child Clinics in Calcutta and told them of her work.

"Three weeks back, before I came here, a woman suffering in the last stages of TB came with her little son, Jamal. When we met, she only asked, 'Mother, as I have got a terrible disease and my days are counted, take my child, give him a home, love him.' I took the child and I told her, 'Well, as long as you are alive, come twice or three times a day, if you like, and see the child.'

"And there was this woman walking at least two or three miles every day. She loved the child in such a heroic way. She would not touch him and begged me, 'Mother, take my child in your arms; you love him. This is what your help has done for Indian mothers. It has helped to draw out of them the best in them." *SAV 135–6*

Words of Mother Teresa

SOMETHING BEAUTIFUL FOR GOD

Mother Teresa electrified the thousands of women assembled at Las Vegas, and made public her deep gratitude for the stream of life-giving foods and medicines channeled through her by Catholic Relief Services. She said she would not plead for aid. People only needed to know the needs of their fellow human beings, she said, and they would respond.

"I don't beg. I have not begged from the time we started the work. But I go to the people—the Hindus, the Mohammedans, and the Christians—and I tell them, 'I have come to give you a chance to do something beautiful for God.' And the people, they want to do something beautiful for God and they come forward."

SAV 136

My Words

A prayer, a modified attitude,
A new sympathy, an action?

_____

_____

_____

_____

_____

_____

WEEK FOURTEEN

The Word

Luke 6:36–38

Be compassionate just as your Father is compassionate. Do
not judge, and you will not be judged; do not condemn, and
you will not be condemned; forgive, and you will be forgiven.
Give, and there will be gifts for you: a full measure, pressed
down, shaken together, and overflowing, will be poured into
your lap; because the standard you use will be the standard
used for you.

Living the Word

When asked what she thought of the city of Las Vegas,
Mother Teresa answered in one word, "Dewali."

Dewali is the yearly Hindu festival of lights to commemorate
the joyful return of Sita, beloved consort of the god Rama. Towns
and villages blossom with candles and strings of electric bulbs.

Mother Teresa made no moral pronouncement, but a perpetual "Dewali" would be as unthinkable to her as to any Indian.

Mother Teresa did carry one souvenir from Las Vegas. To
give her time to meditate before her talk, we drove to the Nevada
desert. She settled by herself near a cactus plant for contemplation. At last she picked up a few of the long cactus spines that
were easily twined into a crown of thorns. This she took back to
Calcutta as a tangible memento of Las Vegas. It was placed on the
head of the crucified Christ hanging behind the altar in the chapel.
Above the crucifix were the words, "I THIRST"–the words to be
placed in every chapel of the Sisters around the world.   *SAV 137*

Words of Mother Teresa

I Thirst

"Just as the seed is meant to be a tree, we are meant to grow in Jesus."–*M.T.*

"I thirst," Jesus said on the Cross when He was deprived of every consolation and left alone, despised and afflicted in body and soul.

As Missionaries of Charity we are called to quench the infinite thirst of Christ–God made Man who suffered, died, yet rose again and is now at the right hand of His Father as well as fully present in the Eucharist, making intercession for us–by:

- a deep life of prayer, contemplation, and penance;
- accepting all suffering, renunciation, and even death;
- as means to understanding better our special call to love and serve Christ in the distressing disguise of the poor.

Const.

My Words

A prayer, a modified attitude,
A new sympathy, an action?

_____

_____

_____

_____

WEEK FIFTEEN

The Word

Psalm 145

Yahweh is trustworthy in all his words,
and upright in all his deeds.
Yahweh supports all who stumble,
lifts up those who are bowed down.

Upright in all that he does,
Yahweh acts only in faithful love.
He is close to all who call upon him,
all who call on him from the heart.

Living the Word

"A beautiful thing happened in Calcutta. Two young people came to see me, Hindu people. They gave me a very big amount of money. 'How did you get so much money?' I asked them. They answered me, 'We got married two days ago. Before our marriage we decided we would not have a big wedding feast and we would not buy wedding clothes. We decided that we would give the money we saved to you to feed the people.'

"In a big Hindu family, a rich family, it's a scandal not to have special wedding clothes and not to have a wedding feast.

" 'Why did you do that?' I asked them. And they answered me, 'Mother, we love each other so much that we wanted to obtain a special blessing from God by making a sacrifice. We wanted to give each other this special gift.'

"Isn't that beautiful? Things like that are happening every day, really beautiful things. We must pull them out. We have to pull out the wonderful things that are happening in the world."

SAV 462

Words of Mother Teresa

GOD HAS HIS OWN WAYS

Though she spoke in Christian terms, Mother Teresa advised all not to condemn or judge other people regarding their paths to God.

"God has His own ways and means to work in the hearts of men, and we do not know how close they are to Him. If the individual thinks and believes that this is the only way to God for her or him, this is the way God comes into their life."   *SAV 476*

My Words

> *A prayer, a modified attitude,*
> *A new sympathy, an action?*

_____
_____
_____
_____
_____
_____
_____
_____
_____
_____
_____

WEEK SIXTEEN

The Word

First Letter of Peter 1:15–21

Be yourselves holy in all your activity, after the model of the
Holy One who calls us, since scripture says, *"Be holy, for I am
holy."* And if you address as Father him who judges without
favouritism according to each individual's deeds, live out the
time of your exile here in reverent awe. For you know that
the price of your ransom from the futile way of life handed
down from your ancestors was paid, not in anything perish-
able like silver or gold, but in precious blood as of a blameless
and spotless lamb, Christ. He was marked out before the
world was made, and was revealed at the final point of time
for your sake. Through him you now have faith in God, who
raised him from the dead and gave him glory for this very
purpose—that your faith and hope should be in God.

Living the Word

I'll never forget during the Bangladesh suffering we had ten
million people in and around Calcutta.

I asked the government of India to allow a number of other
congregations to come to our aid, to help us, because we were
working the whole time.

They allowed them to come; about fifteen or sixteen different
Sisters came to help us, and each one, on leaving Calcutta, said
the same thing, "I received much more than I have given, and I
can never be the same person again, because I have touched
Christ, I have understood what love is. What it is to love and to be
loved!" *MLFP 77*

Words of Mother Teresa

You Are Precious to Me

We need prayer to understand God's love for us.
You have to read that beautiful passage in Isaiah where
God speaks and says:
"I have called you by name. You are mine.
Water will not drown you, fire will not burn you.
I will give up nations for you. You are
precious to me."
We are precious to Him.
That man dying in the street–precious to Him
that millionaire–precious to Him
that sinner–precious to Him,
Because He loves us.   *WTLB 43*

My Words

A prayer, a modified attitude,
A new sympathy, an action?

_____
_____
_____
_____
_____
_____
_____
_____

WEEK SEVENTEEN

The Word

Deuteronomy 6:4–7

Listen, Israel: Yahweh our God is the one, the only Yahweh. You must love Yahweh your God with all your heart, with all your soul, with all your strength. Let the words I enjoin on you today stay in your heart. You shall tell them to your children, and keep on telling them, when you are sitting at home, when you are out and about, when you are lying down and when you are standing up.

Living the Word

"Almighty God," said the rabbi, "it is with a heart full of joy that we have assembled here to give expression to our great joy and render thanksgiving on the occasion of the Silver Jubilee of the Society of the Missionaries of Charity for their humanitarian and selfless work, and through them for the poor of the world."

And now, Psalm 118, verse 24.

"This is the day that the Lord hath made, we will be glad and rejoice therein."

He went on, "And now the day Mother Teresa has hoped for has come. . . . We, the Jews of Calcutta, join in thanksgiving unto the Lord and pray that the Heavenly Father in His mercy preserve Mother Teresa and her band of workers, guard and deliver them from all trouble and sorrow. Hasten the days when the children of men understand that they have one Father, that one God created us all. Then shall the light of universal justice flood the world, and the knowledge of God cover the earth, as the waters cover the sea. Amen." *SAV 279*

Words of Mother Teresa

ALL PEOPLE, OUR BROTHERS AND SISTERS

We have absolutely no difficulty regarding having to work in countries with many faiths, like India. We treat all people as children of God. They are our brothers and sisters. We show great respect to them. . . .

Our work is to encourage these Christians and non-Christians to do works of love. And every work of love, done with a full heart, always brings people closer to God.

If they accept God in their lives, then they are Co-workers.

MLFP 21

My Words

> *A prayer, a modified attitude,*
> *A new sympathy, an action?*

_____

_____

_____

_____

_____

_____

_____

_____

_____

_____

WEEK EIGHTEEN

The Word

Letter of Paul to the Ephesians 2:4–7

God, being rich in faithful love, through the great love with which he loved us, even when we were dead in our sins, brought us to life with Christ—it is through grace that you have been saved—and raised us up with him and gave us a place with him in heaven, in Christ Jesus.

This was to show for all ages to come, through his goodness towards us in Christ Jesus, how extraordinarily rich he is in grace.

Living the Word

The other day I was walking down the street. A man walked up to me and said, "Are you Mother Teresa?" I answered, "Yes." He asked, "Please send some of your Sisters to our house. I'm half blind and my wife is nearly mental. We are simply longing to hear a human voice. . . ."

They had everything, but those two with no one to call their own were so lonely. Their sons and their daughters were quite possibly very far away from them. They are unwanted now, useless so to say, and so they must die of sheer loneliness.

In some places, like in England, we have Co-workers composing small "listening groups." They go to people, ordinary old people's houses, and sit down with them and let them talk and talk. Very old people love to have somebody listen to them even if they have to tell the story of thirty years ago.

To listen, when nobody else wants to listen, is a very beautiful thing. *MLFP 74*

Words of Mother Teresa

THE GREATEST INJUSTICE

We do not know what is the pain of hunger. If we are really able to listen to the voice of God in our hearts, we will realize the suffering of the people. There is so much despair in people's hearts today. . . .

Much of the suffering is the want of that understanding love. People are hungry, not only for bread, but for understanding love. They are naked, not only for clothing, but for that human dignity that has been stolen from them. That is the greatest injustice that is done to the poor, to think of them as good for nothing. We do not treat each one of them as a child of God.

Talk Three

My Words

A prayer, a modified attitude,
A new sympathy, an action?

_____

_____

_____

_____

_____

_____

_____

_____

WEEK NINETEEN

The Word

First Letter of John 3:1–3

> You must see what great love the Father has lavished on
> us
> by letting us be called God's children—
> which is what we are!
> The reason why the world does not acknowledge us
> is that it did not acknowledge him.
> My dear friends, we are already God's children,
> but what we shall be in the future has not yet been re-
> vealed.
> We are well aware that when he appears
> we shall be like him,
> because we shall see Him as he really is.

Living the Word

In our work we have many people whom we call Co-Workers, and I want them to give their hands to serve the people and their hearts to love the people. For unless they come in very close contact with them, it is very difficult for them to know who the poor are. Here in Calcutta especially we have many non-Christians and Christians working together at the Home for the Dying and other places. We have groups who are preparing the bandages and medicine for the lepers.

For example, an Australian came some time ago, and he said that he wanted to give a big donation. But after giving the donation, he said, "That is something outside of me, but I want to give something of me." And now he comes regularly to the Home for the Dying, and he shaves the men and talks to them. He could have spent that time on himself, not just his money. He wanted to give something of himself, and he gives it.   *SBFG 115*

Words of Mother Teresa

CHRIST LOVES WITH MY HEART

As St. Paul has said, "I live no longer I, but Christ lives in me." Christ prays in me, Christ works in me, Christ thinks of me, Christ looks through my eyes, Christ speaks through my words, Christ works with my hands, Christ walks with my feet, Christ loves with my heart. As St. Paul's prayer was, "I belong to Christ, and nothing will separate me from the love of Christ." It was that oneness: oneness with God, oneness with the Master in the Holy Spirit.   *Talk Two*

My Words

A prayer, a modified attitude,
A new sympathy, an action?

WEEK TWENTY

The Word

Matthew 18:1–6

At this time the disciples came to Jesus and said, "Who is the greatest in the kingdom of Heaven?" So he called a little child to him whom he set among them. Then he said, "In truth I tell you, unless you change and become like little children you will never enter the kingdom of Heaven. And so, the one who makes himself as little as this little child is the greatest in the kingdom of Heaven. Anyone who welcomes one little child like this in my name welcomes me. But anyone who is the downfall of one of these little ones who have faith in me would be better drowned in the depths of the sea with a great millstone round his neck."

Living the Word

Some time ago in Calcutta we had great difficulty in getting sugar. And I don't know how the word got around to the children, but a little boy four years old, a Hindu boy, went home and told his parents, "I will not eat sugar for three days. I will give my sugar to Mother Teresa for her children." After three days his father and mother brought him to our house. I had never met them before, and this little one could scarcely pronounce my name. But he knew exactly what he had come to do. He knew that he wanted to share his love. *Talk One*

Words of Mother Teresa

To Show Love

Love begins at home.
If we do not love one another
  whom we see twenty-four hours,
    how can we love those we see only once?
We show love by thoughtfulness
    by kindness
    by sharing joy
    by sharing a smile . . .
through the little things.

A little child has no difficulty in loving,
    has no obstacles to love.
And that is why Jesus said,
    "Unless you become like little children . . ."
                    WTLB 54

My Words

A prayer, a modified attitude,
A new sympathy, an action?

_____

_____
_____
_____
_____

WEEK TWENTY-ONE

The Word

Tobit 4:15-16, 18-19

Do to no one what you would not want done to you.

Give your bread to those who are hungry, and your clothes to those who lack clothing. Of whatever you own in plenty, devote a proportion to almsgiving; and when you give alms, do it ungrudgingly.

Ask advice of every wise person; never scorn any profitable advice. Bless the Lord God in everything: beg him to guide your ways and bring your paths and purposes to their end.

Living the Word

"In India we have thousands of people
    who are hungry.
In one of our houses in Calcutta
    our Sisters daily cook
    for four thousand people,
and the day we don't cook,
    they have nothing to eat.

During the trouble in India,
    when many of our brothers and sisters
    of the same father
    came to India from Pakistan,
these beautiful Indian friends told me,
    'Mother, don't cook for us today.
    Give our food to them.'

For them, it meant going without food
that day."   *MBMS 77*

Words of Mother Teresa

LOVE'S CONTINUITY

We must all fill our hearts with great love. Don't imagine that
love, to be true and burning, must be extraordinary. No—what we
need in our love is the continuity to love the one who loved the
world so much He gave His Son. God is still love, He is still
loving the world. Today God loves the world so much that He
gives you and He gives me to love the world, to be His love and
compassion. The world is hungry for God, and when Jesus came
into the world He wanted to satisfy that hunger. He made himself
the Bread of Life, so small, so fragile, so helpless, and as if that
were not enough, He made himself the hungry one, the naked
one, the homeless one, so that we can satisfy His hunger for love—
for our human love, not something extraordinary but our human
love.   *LIS 35*

My Words

A prayer, a modified attitude,
A new sympathy, an action?

_____

_____

_____

_____

_____

_____

WEEK TWENTY-TWO

The Word

Letter of James 2:14–18

How does it help, my brothers, when someone who has never done a single good act claims to have faith? Will that faith bring salvation? If one of the brothers or one of the sisters is in need of clothes and has not enough food to live on, and one of you says to them, "I wish you well; keep yourself warm and eat plenty," without giving them these bare necessities of life, then what good is that? In the same way faith: if good deeds do not go with it, it is quite dead.

But someone may say: "So you have faith and I have good deeds? Show me this faith of yours without deeds, then! It is by my deeds that I will show you my faith."

Living the Word

A girl came from outside India to join the Missionaries of Charity. We have a rule that new arrivals must go to the Home for the Dying. So I told this girl, "You saw Father during Holy Mass, with what love and care he touched Jesus in the Host. Do the same when you go to the Home for the Dying, because it is the same Jesus you will find there in the broken bodies of our poor." And they went. After three hours the newcomer came back and said to me with a big smile—I have never seen a smile quite like that, "Mother, I have been touching the body of Christ for three hours." And I said to her, "How?" She replied, "When we arrived there, they brought a man who had fallen into a drain and been there for some time. He was covered with wounds and dirt and maggots, and I cleaned him, and I knew I was touching the body of Christ." That was very beautiful. *LIS 56*

Words of Mother Teresa

THERE ARE PEOPLE FALLING DOWN

But if people had that deep respect for the dignity of poor people, I am sure it would be easy for them to come closer to them, and to see that they, too, are the children of God, and that they have as much right to the things of life and of love and of service as anybody else. In these times of development, everybody is in a hurry and everybody's in a rush, and on the way there are people falling down who are not able to compete. These are the ones we want to love and serve and take care of.

SBFG 119

My Words

A prayer, a modified attitude,
A new sympathy, an action?

_____

_____

_____

_____

_____

_____

_____

_____

_____

WEEK TWENTY-THREE

The Word

First Letter of John 1:1–3

the Word of life—
this is our theme.
That life was made visible;
we saw it and are giving our testimony,
declaring to you the eternal life,
which was present to the Father
and has been revealed to us.
We are declaring to you
what we have seen and heard,
so that you too may share our life.
Our life is shared with the Father
and with his Son Jesus Christ.

Living the Word

To relieve the sufferings caused by the Guatemalan earthquake of 1976, Mother Teresa brought a team of the Missionaries of Charity there. She stood in the town of San Pedro where close to one thousand houses had been destroyed and the two churches were jagged shells filled with rubble.

A woman with a walnut-colored, deeply lined face came to talk to us. She told us that she was Cecilia Vasquez, *viuda* (a widow). She told us she had lost her son, daughter-in-law, and little grandson in the earthquake. She was no more than four feet ten inches tall and seemed to be pure Indian. A necklace of coins hung around her neck, and in the center a crucifix.

Cecilia Vasquez held up her crucifix in front of Mother Teresa's eyes. Mother Teresa took hold of the crucifix on her left shoulder and also held it up. They placed them beside each other.

Cecilia Vasquez then threw her arms around Mother Teresa, holding her as though her presence brought consolation in a place marked by sorrow. *SAV 310*

Words of Mother Teresa

She Was All for God

Let us ask our Lady to make our hearts "meek and humble" as her Son's was. It is so very easy to be proud and harsh and selfish, so easy, but we have been created for greater things. How much we can learn from our Lady! She was so humble because she was all for God. She was full of grace. *SBFG 69*

My Words

A prayer, a modified attitude,
A new sympathy, an action?

_____
_____
_____
_____
_____
_____
_____
_____
_____
_____
_____

WEEK TWENTY-FOUR

The Word

John 6:9–13

Andrew, Simon Peter's brother, said, "Here is a small boy with five barley loaves and two fish; but what is that among so many?" Jesus said to them, 'Make the people sit down.' There was plenty of grass there, and as many as five thousand men sat down. Then Jesus took the loaves, gave thanks, and distributed them to those who were sitting there; he then did the same with the fish, distributing as much as they wanted. When they had eaten enough he said to the disciples, "Pick up the pieces left over, so that nothing is wasted." So they picked them up and filled twelve large baskets with scraps left over from the meal of five barley loaves.

Living the Word

We do not accept any government grants; we do not accept church maintenance. We have no salaries, nothing for the work that we do. So we fully depend on Divine Providence. We deal with thousands and thousands of people, and there never has been a day when we have to say to somebody, "Sorry, we don't have."

We cook for about nine thousand people every day. One day the Sister came to me and said, "Mother, there's absolutely nothing. We don't have anything at all." I couldn't answer her. About nine o'clock in the morning a large truck full of bread came to the door. The schools were closed that day. They dropped thousands of loaves inside our walls, and the people had nice bread for two days. How He gives, how He brings things. That is how we are able to care for thousands upon thousands of lepers. *Talk Four*

Words of Mother Teresa

THE WORST DISEASE: THE GREATEST SCOURGE

When the Sisters came to Harlem, they began to visit the old people, the shut-ins who often lived alone. They would do the simple things, clean the rooms, wash the clothes.

Once they came to a door and no one answered. The woman had been dead for five days and no one knew—except for the odor in the hallway. So many are known only by the number on the door.

The worst disease today is not leprosy; it is being unwanted, being left out, being forgotten. The greatest scourge is to forget the next person, to be so suffocated, so to say, with things that we have no time for the lonely Jesus—even a person in our own family who needs us.

Maybe if I had not picked up that one person dying on the street, I would not have picked up the thousands. We must think, Ek, (Bengali for "One") I think Ek, Ek. One, One. That is the way to begin.   *UNPUB*

My Words

> *A prayer, a modified attitude,*
> *A new sympathy, an action?*

_____

_____

_____

_____

_____

WEEK TWENTY-FIVE

The Word

John 16:23–24

When that day comes,
you will not ask me any questions.
In all truth I tell you,
anything you ask from the Father
he will grant in my name.
Until now you have not asked anything in my name.
Ask and you will receive,
and so your joy will be complete.

Living the Word

Many Hindus became Co-Workers in the Home for the Dying and marveled at the attitude of joy that the Sisters brought to their work of caring for the poor. The spirits of the Sisters were buoyed up by the knowledge that they were alleviating the sufferings of those who had been forsaken by all. By their smiles, they were telling the patients that they had reached a place of love and care.

Mother Teresa recounted the effect of the work of the Sisters on a Calcutta man. "A Hindu gentleman stood behind a young Sister who was washing a man just brought into the Home for the Dying. She did not see him. Then, after a time, the man came to me and said, 'I came into this Home empty, full of bitterness and hatred, godless. I am going out full of God. I saw the living love of God through the hands of that Sister, the way she was touching and caring for that man.'"   *SAV 302*

Words of Mother Teresa

Joy, Fruit of the Holy Spirit

Joy is indeed the fruit of the Holy Spirit and a characteristic mark of the Kingdom of God, for God is joy.

–in Bethlehem "Joy," said the angel;
–Christ wanted to share His joy with His Apostles, "that my joy may be with you";
–Joy was the password of the early Christians;
–St. Paul often repeats, "Rejoice in the Lord always; again I say to you, 'Rejoice.' ";
–in return for the great grace of Baptism, the priest tells the newly baptized, "May you serve the Church joyfully."

SAV 303

My Words

A prayer, a modified attitude,
A new sympathy, an action?

_____

_____

_____

_____

_____

_____

_____

WEEK TWENTY-SIX

The Word

Luke 14:12–15

Then he said to his host, "When you give a lunch or a dinner, do not invite your friends or your brothers or your relations or rich neighbours, in case they invite you back and so repay you. No; when you have a party, invite the poor, the crippled, the lame, the blind; then you will be blessed, for they have no means to repay you and so you will be repaid when the upright rise again."

On hearing this, one of those gathered round the table said to him, "Blessed is anyone who will share the meal in the kingdom of God!"

Living the Word

I had the most extraordinary experience with a Hindu family who had eight children. A gentleman came to our house and said, "Mother Teresa, there is a family with eight children, they have not eaten for so long, do something." So I took some rice and I went there immediately. And I saw the children—their eyes shining with hunger. I don't know if you have ever seen hunger. But I have seen it very often. And the mother took the rice, she divided the rice, and she went out. When she came back, I asked her, "Where did you go, what did you do?" And she gave me a very simple answer. "They, the neighbors, are hungry also." What struck me most was that she knew—and who are they? a Muslim family—and she knew. I didn't bring more rice that evening because I wanted them to enjoy the joy of sharing. *Talk One*

Words of Mother Teresa

A Drop in the Ocean

We ourselves feel that what we are doing is just a drop in the ocean. But if that drop were not in the ocean, I think the ocean would be less because of that missing drop. For example, if we didn't have our schools in the slums—they are nothing, they are just little primary schools where we teach the children to love the school and to be clean and so on—if we didn't have these little schools, those children, those thousands of children, would be left in the streets. So we have to choose either to take them and give them just a little, or leave them in the street. It is the same thing for our Home for the Dying and our home for the children.

SBFG 119

My Words

A prayer, a modified attitude,
A new sympathy, an action?

_____

_____

_____

_____

_____

_____

_____

_____

WEEK TWENTY-SEVEN

The Word

Letter of Paul to the Romans 14:12–13, 17–19

It is to God, then, that each of us will have to give an account of himself.

Let us each stop passing judgement, therefore, on one another and decide instead that none of us will place obstacles in any brother's way, or anything that can bring him down.

It is not eating and drinking that make the kingdom of God, but the saving justice, the peace and the joy brought by the Holy Spirit. It is the person who serves Christ in these things that will be approved by God and respected by everyone. So then, let us be always seeking the ways which lead to peace and the ways in which we can support one another.

Living the Word

In the house of the dying
   there is so much suffering of the heart.
There is no one,
   no one to love them,
but the Sisters love them.
They smile and wash and clean them;
they are so good,
   a presence of peace in the midst of
   disease, cancer, T.B., and other things!

"One day a man was brought in
   screaming and yelling. . . . His pain was intense. . . .

He was given morphine and love in generous doses,
and he was told of the sufferings of One
who loved him very much.

Gradually he began to listen and to accept love.
On his last day he refused the morphine
  because he wanted to be united to the One
  who saved him."   *MBMS 65*

Words of Mother Teresa

EVERYTHING IS "THE FRUIT OF LOVE"

To love means to do everything for Jesus. I get the strength
to do what I have to do from the Eucharist—daily Holy Communion. This is why Jesus made Himself the Bread of Life: to be our
life, to give us life.

It is His love that moves us. Everything I do is the fruit of
love, because my life is an expression of love. At this moment as I
address you, I do it for Jesus, so I am speaking to Jesus. Truly
there can be no separation between action and meditation, because each act, each gesture, every moment is done with Him. He
said so Himself, and Jesus does not fool us: Whatever you did to
others, you did to Me. When I live, work, talk with my Sisters, I
talk, work, and live with Jesus. With the poor, the sick, the lepers,
and the dying, I am with Jesus. So I live twenty-four hours of the
day with Jesus; to Him I have dedicated my life, my heart, my
whole being, and my work.   *CoW-N*

My Words

> *A prayer, a modified attitude,*
> *A new sympathy, an action?*

_____

_____

_____

_____

_____

WEEK TWENTY-EIGHT

The Word

Letter of Paul to the Romans 12:17–21

Never pay back evil with evil, but *bear in mind the ideals that all regard with respect.* As much as is possible, and to the utmost of your ability, be at peace with everyone. Never try to get revenge: leave that, my dear friends, to the Retribution. As scripture says: *Vengeance is mine—I will pay them back,* the Lord promises. And more: *If your enemy is hungry, give him something to eat; if thirsty, something to drink. By this, you will be heaping red-hot coals on his head.* Do not be mastered by evil, but master evil with good.

Living the Word

We have a home for the alcoholics in Melbourne, a home for homeless alcoholics.

One of them was very badly hurt by another. Then I thought this would be a case for the police. So we sent for the police, and the police came and asked that gentleman, "Who did that to you?"

He started telling all kinds of lies, but he wouldn't tell the truth, he wouldn't give the name, and the policeman had to go away without doing anything.

Then I asked him, "Why did you not tell the police who did that to you?"

He looked at me and said, "His suffering is not going to lessen my suffering."

He hid the name of his brother to save him from suffering.

How beautiful and how great is the love of our people, and this is a continual miracle of love that's spread among our people. We call them poor, but they are rich in love!   *MLFP 71*

Words of Mother Teresa

THE LIMIT OF LOVE—THE CROSS

"Love one another, even as I have loved you." These words should be not only a light to us, but also a flame consuming the selfishness that prevents the growth of holiness. Jesus loved us to the end, to the very limit of love, the Cross. Love must come from within—from our union with Christ—an outpouring of our love for God. Loving should be as normal to us as living and breathing, day after day until our death. The Little Flower said, "When I act and think with charity, I feel it is Jesus who works within me. The closer I am united with Him, the more I love all the other dwellers in Carmel." *LIS 37*

My Words

> *A prayer, a modified attitude,*
> *A new sympathy, an action?*

_____

_____

_____

_____

_____

_____

_____

_____

_____

WEEK TWENTY-NINE

The Word

First Letter of John 4:9–10

This is the revelation of God's love for us,
that God sent his only Son into the world
that we might have life through him.
Love consists in this:
it is not we who loved God,
but God loved us and sent his Son
to expiate our sins.

Living the Word

Mother Teresa spoke at many sessions of the 1976 Eucharistic Congress in Philadelphia. At the last minute she was asked to speak to a large gathering of young people.

"Today, in young people of the world, Jesus lives His passion, in the suffering, in the hungry, the handicapped young people.

"Those thousands who die not only for a piece of bread, but for a little bit of love, of recognition. That is a station of the Cross. Are you there?

"And young people, when they fall, as Jesus fell again and again for us, are we there as Simon Cyrene to pick them up, to pick up the Cross?

Afterward a priest remarked that the talk was perfect for the occasion. The young people had been stunned when Ellen Potts, a twenty-year-old leader of youth participation in the Congress, had been struck down by leukemia. Mother Teresa was unaware of this.

"I do not know what made me talk like that about the Cross. It suddenly came to me."   *SAV 325*

Words of Mother Teresa

LET HIM PRAY IN ME

When times come when we can't pray, it is very simple: If Jesus is in my heart, let Him pray, let me allow Him to pray in me, talk to His Father in the silence of my heart. Since I cannot speak—He will speak; since I cannot pray—He will pray. That's why often we should say, "Jesus in my heart, I believe in Your faithful love for me, I love you." And often we should be in that unity with Him and allow Him, and when we have nothing to give—let us give Him that nothingness. When we cannot pray—let us give that inability to Him.

There is one more reason to let Him pray in us to the Father. Let us ask Him to pray in us, for no one knows the Father better than He. No one can pray better than Jesus.   *Talk Two*

My Words

> *A prayer, a modified attitude,*
> *A new sympathy, an action?*

_____

_____

_____

_____

_____

_____

_____

_____

WEEK THIRTY

The Word

John 10:14–17

> I am the good shepherd;
> I know my own
> and my own know me,
> just as the Father knows me,
> and I know the Father;
> and I lay down my life for my sheep.
> And there are other sheep I have
> that are not of this fold,
> and I must lead these too.
> They too will listen to my voice,
> and there will be only one flock,
> one shepherd.
> The Father loves me,
> because I lay down my life
> in order to take it up again.

Living the Word

To a friend who is sorely ill and has asked for her prayers, she writes: "Your name is up on the wall, at the entrance to the Motherhouse Chapel, and the whole house will pray for you, including me. St. Peter will be surprised at the avalanche of prayer for you, and will, I am sure, make you well soon. Maybe, though, you are ready to go 'home' to God. If so, He will be very happy to open the 'door' for you and let you in for all eternity." Then, in her inimitable way, she adds, "If you go 'home' before me, give Jesus and His mother my love."   *GFG 7–8*

Words of Mother Teresa

THEY HAVE THEIR DIGNITY

Today our poor of the world are looking up at you. Do you look back at them with compassion? Do you have compassion for the people who are hungry? They are hungry not only for bread and for rice, they are hungry to be recognized as human beings. They are hungry for you to know that they have their dignity, that they want to be treated as you are treated. They are hungry for love.   *MDV 23*

My Words

A prayer, a modified attitude,
A new sympathy, an action?

_____

_____

_____

_____

_____

_____

_____

_____

_____

_____

_____

_____

_____

WEEK THIRTY-ONE

The Word

Genesis 1:26–27

God said, "Let us make man in our own image, in the likeness of ourselves, and let them be masters of the fish of the sea, the birds of heaven, the cattle, all the wild animals and all the creatures that creep along the ground."

God created man in the image of himself,
in the image of God he created him,
male and female he created them.

Living the Word

Before a king and a hall filled with academics, diplomats, politicians, members of the armed forces in full uniform, and an immense press corps, Mother Teresa received the ultimate accolade, the Nobel Prize for Peace. It was December 10, 1979.

Her white sari shone under the spotlights as she asked the whole assembly to join her in the prayer attributed to everyone's saint, Francis, the poor man of Assisi. They intoned in unison from cards she had brought with her, "Lord, make me a channel of your peace; where there is hatred, let me sow love, where there is injury, pardon. . . ."

Awaiting Mother Teresa on the dais of the Great Hall of the University of Oslo was Professor John Sannes, Chairman of the Nobel Committee.

"As a description of Mother Teresa's life's work we might select the slogan that a previous Nobel Peace Prize Laureate,

Albert Schweitzer, adopted as the leitmotif for his own work: 'Veneration for Life.' " *SAV 2, 402–3*

Words of Mother Teresa

THE IMAGE OF GOD IS ON THAT UNBORN CHILD

The Good News was peace to all of goodwill, and this is something that we all want–peace of heart. And God loved the world so much that He gave His Son.

As soon as Jesus came in her life, Mary immediately went in haste to give that Good News. As she came into the house of her cousin, the child–the unborn child–the child in the womb of Elizabeth–leaped with joy. He was, that little unborn child, the first messenger of peace. He recognized the Prince of Peace.

I feel the greatest destroyer of peace today is abortion, because it is a direct war, a direct killing, direct murder by the mother herself. We read in the Scripture, for God says very clearly, "Even if a mother could forget her child, I will not forget you. I have carved you in the palm of my hand." We are carved in the palm of His hand, so close to Him. That unborn child has been carved in the hand of God. *Talk One*

My Words

A prayer, a modified attitude,
A new sympathy, an action?

_____

_____

_____

_____

WEEK THIRTY-TWO

The Word

Isaiah 57:15

Thus says the High and Exalted One
who lives eternally
and whose name is holy,
"I live in the holy heights
but I am with the contrite and humble,
to revive the spirit of the humble,
to revive the heart of the contrite."

Living the Word

Mother Teresa did not take herself too seriously and never
stood on her dignity. She would squat unself-consciously on the
carpeted area at an airport terminal to have a chance to talk to the
Sisters as they sat around her. When she began using the Indian
trains to visit the first houses of the Sisters, she would swing
herself into the capacious luggage rack for a few hours' sleep.
That was before she was given a free pass on the Indian railway.
It was probably the rail pass that prodded her into suggesting to
Indian Air Lines that they take her on as a stewardess. She could
serve meals and do the humble necessary work in return for free
travel throughout India to visit the Sisters. She did not get the
job, but instead was, in 1973, given a free pass on Indian Air Lines.

SAV 446

Words of Mother Teresa

A LITTLE PENCIL IN GOD'S HAND

I think this is something very, very important for each one of us, for you and for me—to be in love with Christ. And how do we show that love for Christ? By putting that love into action. Because every work of love brings us more and more to Christ, to Jesus, makes us more and more Christlike.

What is important is, am I really, really a Co-Worker of Christ? Do I really, truly put into life His love? Am I a little instrument? I always say I am a little pencil in the hands of God. He does the thinking, He does the writing, He does everything. Sometimes it is a broken pencil! It needs to be sharpened a little more! Be a little instrument so that He can use you, anytime, anywhere. *Talk Four*

My Words

A prayer, a modified attitude,
A new sympathy, an action?

_____

_____

_____

_____

_____

_____

WEEK THIRTY-THREE

The Word

First Letter of John 4:11–14

My dear friends,
if God loved us so much,
we too should love each other.
No one has ever seen God,
but as long as we love each other
God remains in us
and his love comes to its perfection in us.
This is the proof that we remain in him
and he in us,
that he has given us a share in his Spirit.
We ourselves have seen and testify
that the Father sent his Son
as Saviour of the world.

Living the Word

The poor are very wonderful people. One evening we went out and we picked up four people from the street. And one of them was in a most terrible condition. And I told the Sisters, "You take care of the other three; I will take care of this one that looks worse." So I did for her all that my love can do. I put her in bed, and there was such a beautiful smile on her face. She took hold of my hand, as she said only, "Thank you"–and she died.

I could not help but examine my conscience before her. And I asked, "What would I say if I were in her place?" And my answer was very simple. I would have tried to draw a little attention to myself. I would have said, "I am hungry, I am dying, I am cold, I am in pain," or something. But she gave me much more–she gave me her grateful love. And she died with a smile on her face.

Talk One

Words of Mother Teresa

GREATNESS OF THE POOR

I wonder what the world would be like
if there were not these great people who continually
    suffer,
    suffer with such dignity and love.

The dying man who said to one of our Sisters,
    "I am going home to God."
He did not curse anybody.
He did not say anything about his difficulties,
    only, "I am going home to God."
Then he closed his eyes
and went home.
Just as simple and beautiful as that.
He went home to Jesus.
He went home to see the face of God. . . .

We don't realize the greatness of the poor
and how much they give us.   *WTLB 69*

My Words

A prayer, a modified attitude,
A new sympathy, an action?

_____

_____

_____

_____

_____

_____

WEEK THIRTY-FOUR

The Word

Matthew 18:19–20

In truth I tell you once again, if two of you on earth agree to ask anything at all, it will be granted to you by my Father in heaven. For where two or three meet in my name, I am there among them.

Living the Word

When a few of us were traveling with her, Mother Teresa involved us in prayer. We would recite the rosary, each person taking one of the mysteries. Once when we were driving across Minnesota, we joined in prayer for an unemployed man to find a job. After the prayer Mother Teresa said, "Let us thank God for his job." Mother Teresa took it for granted that, "Whatever you ask, believe you will receive it and it will come to you." The man received the job.

To travel with Mother Teresa was to experience the presence of a person who was completely recollected. On one occasion we were driven at breakneck speed through the heart of Chicago to catch a plane. Patty Kump and I caught our breath as we made swift turns in traffic, barely grazing a taxi and shooting forward like a rocket as soon as the light changed to green. Mother Teresa's countenance never changed; she sat calmly with her rosary beads in her hands, praying.   *SAV 443*

Words of Mother Teresa

START WITH THE "OUR FATHER"

If we can bring prayer into the family, the family will stay together. They will love one another. Just get together for five minutes. Start with the Our Father, that's all! Or we can say,

"My Lord, I love You.
My God, I am sorry.
My God, I believe in You.
My God, I trust You.
Help us to love one another
as You love us."

That is where your strength will come from.   *WTLB 57*

My Words

A prayer, a modified attitude,
A new sympathy, an action?

_____
_____
_____
_____
_____
_____
_____
_____
_____

WEEK THIRTY-FIVE

The Word

2 Corinthians 12:9–10

"My grace is enough for you: for power is at full stretch in weakness." It is, then, about my weaknesses that I am happiest of all to boast, so that the power of Christ may rest upon me; and that is why I am glad of weaknesses, insults, constraints, persecutions and distress for Christ's sake. For it is when I am weak that I am strong.

Living the Word

A reporter asked her about a much-used photograph of Mother Teresa holding a Bengali child. Her expression is one of profound grief, possibly mingled with anger.

"Yes," she commented, "I was angry. The child was very sick and they were leaving him behind. That's why I look angry. I picked him up and we took him to Shishu Bhavan, our children's home in Calcutta. We did everything, but he died in two weeks."

"What makes you feel sad?" came from another reporter.

"Things like this. A woman came to us in Calcutta with a sick baby in her arms. We were going to do our best, and she gave me the little one. But the baby died right there in my arms. I saw that woman's face as she stood there, and I felt the way she did."

"What is your purpose in picking up dying people?"

"Each one is the homeless Christ, no?"

"Is Christ partial to the poor, Mother Teresa?"

"Christ is not partial. He is hungry for our love, and to give us the chance to put our love into a living action, He makes Himself the poor one, the hungry one, the naked one. He said it clearly, 'I was hungry and you fed Me; I was naked and you clothed Me. You did it to Me.'"   *SAV 306*

Words of Mother Teresa

WE HAVE TO DIVE INTO POVERTY

To know the problem of poverty intellectually is not to understand it. It is not by reading, talking, walking in the slum . . . that we come to understand it and discover what it has of bad and of good. We have to dive into it, live it, share it.

Only by being one with us has Jesus redeemed us. We are allowed to do the same; all the desolation of the poor people, not only their material poverty but their spiritual poverty, must be redeemed.   *SAV 474*

My Words

A prayer, a modified attitude,
A new sympathy, an action?

_____
_____
_____
_____
_____
_____
_____
_____
_____
_____
_____

WEEK THIRTY-SIX

The Word

Matthew 5:9, 43–46, 48

Blessed are the peacemakers:
they shall be recognised as children of God.

You have heard how it was said, *You will love your neigh-bour* and hate your enemy. But I say this to you, love your enemies and pray for those who persecute you; so that you may be children of your Father in heaven, for he causes his sun to rise on the bad as well as the good, and sends down rain to fall on the upright and the wicked alike.

"You must therefore set no bounds to your love, just as your heavenly Father sets none to His."

Living the Word

To Corrymeela ("Hill of Harmony" in Gaelic), a community of reconciliation, Mother Teresa was invited in July 1981. The meeting was held in a large tent overlooking the sea fifty miles north of Belfast.

Mother Teresa came into contact with people on both sides of the conflict in Northern Ireland. She was in the midst of people mourning men, women, and children who had been cut down in nearly ten years of sporadic violence. Some had family members in prison. The violence, sparked by the 1972 Bloody Sunday when soldiers killed thirteen unarmed civil rights demonstrators, was a long-term effect of the unhealed wound of the partition of the island nation. She talked in gospel terms of love and forgiveness.

Mairead Corrigan, who had shared the Nobel Peace Prize with Betty Williams, wrote, "Mother Teresa said nothing I had not heard before or read from the gospels, but she brings the whole thing to life. I think what makes Mother Teresa's words so effective is that she is living out her words in her life."

SAV 453–4

Words of Mother Teresa

To Forgive Out of Love, to Forget Out of Humility

In His passion Jesus taught us how to forgive out of love, how to forget out of humility. So let us examine our hearts and see if there is any unforgiven hurt–any unforgotten bitterness! The quickest and surest way is the "tongue"–use it for the good of others. If you think well of others, you will also speak well of others and to others. From the abundance of the heart the mouth speaketh. If your heart is full of love you will speak of love. If you forgive others the wrong they have done, your heavenly Father will also forgive you, but if you do not forgive others, then the wrongs you have done will not be forgiven by your Father. It is easy to love those who are far away. It isn't always easy to love those who are right next to us.   *CoW–N*

My Words

A prayer, a modified attitude,
A new sympathy, an action?

WEEK THIRTY-SEVEN

The Word

First Letter of John 3:16–19

> This is the proof of love,
> that he laid down his life for us,
> and we too ought to lay down our lives for our brothers.
> If anyone is well off in worldly possessions
> and sees his brother in need
> but closes his heart to him,
> how can the love of God be remaining in him?
> Children,
> our love must be not just words or mere talk,
> but something active and genuine.
> This will be the proof that we belong to the truth.

Living the Word

In a city northeast of Calcutta, Mother Teresa acquired a piece of land for a Home for the Destitute Dying. It happened that in that locality many families had built new homes, and they organized the opposition to having the destitute in their midst. A wall was erected to block Mother Teresa and the Sisters from coming into the section. When supporters of Mother Teresa's work tried to remove the barrier, there were beatings.

On the day of Mother Teresa's arrival, she stood at the barrier and spoke to the people. Word had been spread that she would bring lepers into the neighborhood. She explained that this was untrue, but that she would be bringing the poor and homeless. Mother Teresa made her entreaties on behalf of the rejected, but her way was still barred. She decided to leave that locality, saying, "I'm sorry for you people. Later on you will regret it. You have not rejected me, but you have rejected God's poor." She complied with the people's "Go back," and left. One could picture her shaking the dust of that locality from her sandals.

SAV 419

Words of Mother Teresa

THOSE WHOSE TEARS HAVE RUN DRY

My true community is the poor—their security is my security, their health is my health. My home is among the poor, and not only the poor, but the poorest of them: the people no one will go near because they are filthy and suffering from contagious diseases, full of germs and vermin-infested—the people who can't go to church because they can't go out naked—the people who can no longer eat because they haven't the strength—the people who lie down in the street, knowing they are going to die, while others look away and pass them by—the people who no longer cry because their tears have run dry! The Lord wants me exactly where I am—He will provide the answers. *LWB 26*

My Words

A prayer, a modified attitude,
A new sympathy, an action?

_____

_____

_____

_____

_____

WEEK THIRTY-EIGHT

The Word

First Letter of John 5:20

> We are well aware also that the Son of God has come,
> and has given us understanding
> so that we may know the One who is true.
> We are in the One who is true
> as we are in his Son, Jesus Christ.
> He is the true God
> and this is eternal life.

Living the Word

After a talk at St. Olaf's church in Minneapolis, there was time for questioning.

A woman in a wheelchair surprised the congregation by raising her hand to ask a question. She was a victim of cerebral palsy, and her whole body moved convulsively without letup. The handicap affected her speech, but at last it was clear that she was asking Mother Teresa what people like her could do for others or for the world.

Mother Teresa did not hesitate. "You can do the most," she replied. "You can do more than any of us because your suffering is united with the suffering of Christ on the Cross, and it brings strength to all of us. You pray the work with us."

After the service the woman, Mary Wojciak, was brought to the sacristy where, weeping with joy, she embraced Mother Teresa. She became a member of the "Sick and Suffering Co-Workers of Mother Teresa" and composed a prayer that concluded in this way: "O Merciful Lord, let us suffer without regret, for in Your will and our gracious acceptance of that holy will, lives our eternal destiny." She died shortly afterward. *SAV 371*

Words of Mother Teresa

Peace Is His Companion Now

So your beloved brother has died. You must not grieve for him. He is with God. We all have to go there, home to God. And there is no unhappiness there, but all *Shanti* (peace), a real *Shanti Nagar* (town of peace). So why should you be sad? *Shanti* is his companion now.   *UNPUB*

My Words

> *A prayer, a modified attitude,*
> *A new sympathy, an action?*

_____

_____

_____

_____

_____

_____

_____

_____

_____

_____

_____

_____

_____

WEEK THIRTY-NINE

The Word

Letter of Paul to the Philippians 2:5–9

Make your own the mind of Christ Jesus:
Who, being in the form of God,
did not count equality with God
something to be grasped.

But he emptied himself,
taking the form of a slave,
becoming as human beings are;

and being in every way like a human being,
he was humbler yet,
even to accepting death, death on a cross.

Living the Word

People seem to think, if they thought about it at all, that Mother Teresa was barely human, indefatigable. Though she did not intrude her human needs on others, she was deeply human. Out of her boundless grief, when she knew her mother's health was failing and it was certain that she and her sister would never leave Albania, she wrote, "They are all His more than mine. You don't know what this sacrifice of not seeing my mother has obtained for my Sisters." Later, as her mother's strength was failing, Mother Teresa wrote, "Her and my sacrifice will bring us closer to God."

When an interviewer asked if she would not have wanted children of her own, she answered, "Naturally, naturally. That is the sacrifice." She stated publicly that she needed to go to confession like anyone else and that she could make mistakes, even in the placement of Sisters. "I can make mistakes," she would say, "but God does not make mistakes." *SAV 448*

Words of Mother Teresa

GOD CANNOT FILL WHAT IS FULL

Letter to a priest who complained of feeling empty and drained:

"You have said 'Yes' to Jesus—and He has taken you at your word. The word of God became man—poor; your word to God became Jesus—poor. And so this terrible emptiness you experience. God cannot fill what is full—He can fill only emptiness—deep poverty—and your 'Yes' is the beginning of being or becoming empty. It is not how much we really 'have' to give—but how empty we are—so that we can receive fully in our life and let Him live His life in us." *SAV 448*

My Words

A prayer, a modified attitude,
A new sympathy, an action?

_____

_____

_____

_____

_____

_____

_____

WEEK FORTY

The Word

Proverbs 21:13

Whoever refuses to listen to the cry of the weak
will in turn plead and not be heard.

Proverbs 22:2

Rich and poor rub shoulders,
Yahweh has made them both.

Living the Word

What I see today are so many broken families, so much
sorrow, so much pain. A man or a woman is always coming to us
to ask for prayers because the family has been broken. Yet among
our poor people in India family love is strong.

I picked up a little girl, dirty and miserable, and I brought her
to Shishu Bhavan, our children's home. We gave her fresh clothing
and fed her. But the next day she disappeared. Some time later she
was brought in again. The dirt was washed off; she had good food
and a clean bed. But again she disappeared. I asked a Sister to look
out for her. Finally she found the child. She was sitting under a
tree, and the mother was cooking something over two stones.
Sometimes the mother would hug the child. Under that tree was
home to that child. And she was happier there than with us where
she had everything. *Talk Six*

Words of Mother Teresa

Do the Poor Have Health Insurance?

When our Sisters went to Paris to begin the work, the Church leaders explained about health insurance. They were going to have all the Sisters insured and they had the forms ready.

I said, "No, that is not for us." Everybody was shocked and tried to make me change my mind. "Do the poor that we work with have health insurance?" That settled it.

If we live with the poor, we must share their poverty and depend on the providence of Almighty God for His help. That is our faith. *UNPUB*

My Words

A prayer, a modified attitude,
A new sympathy, an action?

_____
_____
_____
_____
_____
_____
_____
_____
_____
_____
_____

WEEK FORTY-ONE

The Word

First Letter of Peter 3:18, 21, 22

Christ himself died once and for all for sins, the upright for the sake of the guilty, to lead us to God. In the body he was put to death, in the spirit he was raised to life, and, in the spirit, he went to preach to the spirits in prison.

It is the baptism corresponding to this water which saves you now—not the washing off of physical dirt but the pledge of a good conscience given to God through the resurrection of Jesus Christ, who has entered heaven and is at God's right hand, with angels, ruling forces and powers subject to him.

Living the Word

"How can a merciful God," asked a newspaperman, "allow such suffering—children dying of hunger, people killed in earthquakes in Guatemala? What can you say to that?"

Mother Teresa spoke softly and meditatively.

"All that suffering—where would the world be without it? It is innocent suffering, and that is the same as the suffering of Jesus. He suffered for us, and all the innocent suffering is joined to His in the redemption. It is co-redemption. That is helping to save the world from worse things."

An earnest young woman queried, "Isn't it next to impossible to be a Christian in our society?"

"Yes," she replied. "It is hard. And we cannot do it without help, without prayer. We Catholics have the body of Christ. This gives us the strength we need. Jesus comes to us in the form of bread to show us His love for us, and He makes Himself the hungry one so that we can feed Him. He is always there, the hungry one, the homeless one, and the naked one." *SAV 307*

Words of Mother Teresa

PRAYER, SOMETHING TO LOOK FORWARD TO

Prayer is not meant to be a torture, not meant to make us feel uneasy, is not meant to trouble us. It is something to look forward to, to talk to my Father, to talk to Jesus, the one to whom I belong: body, soul, mind, heart.

And this is what makes us contemplatives in the heart of the world, for we are twenty-four hours then in His presence: in the hungry, in the naked, in the homeless, in the unwanted, unloved, uncared for, for Jesus said, "Whatever you do to the least of my brethren, you do it to me."

Therefore doing it to Him, we are praying the work; for in doing it with Him, doing it for Him, doing it to Him we are loving Him, and in loving Him we come more and more into that oneness with Him and we allow Him to live His life in us. And this living of Christ in us is holiness. *Talk Two*

My Words

A prayer, a modified attitude,
A new sympathy, an action?

_____

_____

_____

_____

_____

_____

WEEK FORTY-TWO

The Word

Second Letter of Paul to the Corinthians 1:5–7, 20

Just as the sufferings of Christ overflow into our lives, so too does the encouragement we receive through Christ. So if we have hardships to undergo, this will contribute to your encouragement and your salvation; if we receive encouragement, this is to gain for you the encouragement which enables you to bear with perseverance the same sufferings as we do. So our hope for you is secure in the knowledge that you share the encouragement we receive, no less than the sufferings we bear. For in him is found the yes to all God's promises and therefore it is "through him" that we answer "Amen" to give praise to God.

Living the Word

On Christmas Eve 1985 we saw Mother Teresa help a small man up the steps into a hospice in New York's Greenwich Village. He had been released to the care of the Sisters so that he would not pass his last days behind prison walls. The hospice was called Gift of Love and was run by four Missionaries of Charity. It was for patients in the final stages of the deadly affliction of AIDS.

Mother Teresa explained why she wanted the opening to be on Christmas Eve. "Then Jesus was born, so I wanted to help them to be born again in joy and love and peace. We are hoping that they will be able to live and die in peace by getting tender love and care because each one of them is Jesus in a distressing disguise."

The opening of the AIDS hospice seemed to open many hearts. "So many people have come forward," Mother Teresa related. "It is beautiful." *SAV 492–3*

Words of Mother Teresa

SAY "YES" TO JESUS

We have only to say "Yes" to Him. This is what I pray for you, I really pray that you really be His love, His compassion, His tenderness.

With this AIDS disease I think that God is telling us something more. God is giving us something so that we can show that tender love, that concern. In this troubled world this sickness has come to teach us something, to open our eyes to the need of the tender love that we all have and that has been forgotten, been pushed out. I remember when those people with AIDS were in jail and we had to sit in that jail, one said, "I don't want to die here, I don't want to die in jail." And then, thank God, we prayed and prayed to Our Lady, and then we called the governor and the mayor. A big miracle, I believe, happened. In the United States everything takes a long time to get all the papers in order, but within a few hours the men came out of prison.   *Talk Four*

My Words

A prayer, a modified attitude,
A new sympathy, an action?

_____

_____

_____

_____

_____

_____

WEEK FORTY-THREE

The Word

Luke 12:16–21

He told them a parable. "There was once a rich man who, having had a good harvest from his land, thought to himself, 'What am I to do? I have not enough room to store my crops.' Then he said, 'This is what I will do: I will pull down my barns and build bigger ones, and store all my grain and my goods in them, and I will say to my soul: My soul, you have plenty of good things laid by for many years to come; take things easy, eat, drink, have a good time.' But God said to him, 'Fool! This very night the demand will be made for your soul; and this hoard of yours, whose will it be then?' " So it is when someone stores up treasure for himself instead of becoming rich in the sight of God."

Living the Word

There was a lady, an Indian, a very rich lady, who came to see me. "Mother Teresa," she said, "I love you very much and I want to do something for you."

I said, "Yes. That would be most welcome."

"I have a great love for beautiful saris," she told me. "I always buy very expensive saris." Her saris cost eight hundred rupees. (Ours cost eight rupees.)

Then she told me that she bought a new sari every month.

So I said, "Let your saris share in the work. The next time you go to the market to buy a sari, you buy a sari of seven hundred, then six hundred, then five hundred. The rest can go for saris for the poor. Then each, less, less, until you come down to a sari of one hundred rupees." I didn't allow her to go lower.

For her, that was a big sacrifice. But it brought so much joy to her, and to the whole family, for they all had a share in it.

Talk Four

Words of Mother Teresa

GOD DOES NOT FORCE HIMSELF

Faith is a gift of God,
  but God does not force himself.

Christians, Muslims, Hindus, believers and nonbelievers
  have the opportunity with us to do works of love,
  have the opportunity with us to share the joy of
    loving and come to realize God's presence.
Hindus become better Hindus.
Catholics become better Catholics.
Muslims become better Muslims.   *WTLB 35*

My Words

A prayer, a modified attitude,
A new sympathy, an action?

WEEK FORTY-FOUR

The Word

Matthew 13:44

The kingdom of Heaven is like treasure hidden in a field which someone has found; he hides it again, goes off in his joy, sells everything he owns and buys the field.

Living the Word

When Mother Teresa found a group of Co-Workers dispirited, she would raise their spirits with a joke. One joke concerned a traveler whose car broke down at the edge of a lonely, barren region. The only refuge was a monastery and the only transport the monks could offer the man was a donkey. The traveler insisted on continuing his journey, so the monks explained that to manage the animal, the man must remember to say, "Amen, Amen," when he wanted it to stop, but, "Thank God, thank God," when he wanted it to go forward.

All went well until a precipice loomed before him, and the nervous man remembered just in time to shout "Amen, Amen." The donkey stopped at the very edge of the precipice. Then the man said fervently, "Thank God, thank God," and over he went. We burst out laughing because in a way it was a joke on Mother Teresa herself, who was saying, "Thank God," everywhere and at all times.   *SAV 446*

Words of Mother Teresa

THE JOY OF CHRIST RISEN

Joy is prayer–Joy is strength–Joy is love–Joy is a net of love by which you can catch souls. God loves a cheerful giver. He or she gives most who gives with joy. The best way to show our gratitude to God and the people is to accept everything with joy. A joyful heart is the normal result of a heart burning with love. Never let anything so fill you with sorrow as to make you forget the joy of Christ Risen.   *SBFG 68*

My Words

> *A prayer, a modified attitude,*
> *A new sympathy, an action?*

_____

_____

_____

_____

_____

_____

_____

_____

_____

_____

_____

WEEK FORTY-FIVE

The Word

Letter of Paul to the Romans 6:4–6

By our baptism into his death we were buried with him, so that as Christ was raised from the dead by the Father's glorious power, we too should begin living a new life. If we have been joined to him by dying a death like his, so we shall be by a resurrection like his; realising that our former self was crucified with him, so that the self which belonged to sin should be destroyed and we should be freed from the slavery of sin.

Living the Word

Thousands of people suffering from AIDS walk the streets. I opened our first house for AIDS patients in New York City. Already fourteen are dead because there is no cure for this disease.

One patient had to leave our home to go to the hospital. When I visited him, he said to me, "Mother Teresa, you are my friend. I want to talk to you alone."

What did he say after twenty-five years of being away from God? "When I get the terrible pain in my head, I share it with Jesus and suffer as He did when He was crowned with thorns. When I get the terrible pain in my back, I share it with Him when He was scourged at the pillar, and when I get the pain in my hands and feet, I share it with Him when He was nailed to the Cross. I ask you to take me home. I want to die with you."

I got permission and took him to our home, Gift of Love, and took him into the chapel. I never heard anyone talk to Jesus like this man talked to Him, so tenderly, so full of love. Three days later he died.   *CoW–N*

Words of Mother Teresa

A Sign of His Love

Suffering shared with Christ's passion is a wonderful gift. Man's most beautiful gift is that he can share in the passion of Christ. Yes, a gift and a sign of His love, because this is how His Father proved that He loved the world, by giving His Son to die for us.

And so in Christ it was proved that the greatest gift is Love, because suffering was how He paid for our sin.   *CoW–N*

My Words

A prayer, a modified attitude,
A new sympathy, an action?

_____
_____
_____
_____
_____
_____
_____
_____
_____
_____
_____

WEEK FORTY-SIX

The Word

First Letter of Paul to the Corinthians 1:4–9

I am continually thanking God about you, for the grace of God which you have been given in Christ Jesus; in him you have been richly endowed in every kind of utterance and knowledge, so firmly has witness to Christ taken root in you. And so you are not lacking in any gift as you wait for our Lord Jesus Christ to be revealed; he will continue to give you strength till the very end, so that you will be irreproachable on the Day of our Lord Jesus Christ. You can rely on God, who has called you to be partners with his Son Jesus Christ our Lord.

Living the Word

I remember one day I visited a lady who had a very bad cancer. She had little children. I didn't know which was the greater agony, the agony of the body or the agony of leaving the children.

She was really dying, so I said to her, "You know this is but the kiss of Jesus. See, Jesus loves you so much, you have come so close to Jesus on the Cross, that He can kiss you."

She joined her hands and said, "Mother Teresa, please tell Jesus to stop kissing me."

Sometimes you have to say to Jesus, "Please stop kissing me." Say it to Him. And when you feel generous, and you do not have too many things to offer up, say, "Jesus, keep on kissing me."

Talk Four

Words of Mother Teresa

LEARN TO PRAY BY LOVING

It was the apostles who asked Jesus, "Jesus, teach us how to pray"—because they saw Him so often pray and they knew that He was talking to His Father. What those hours of prayer must have been—we know only from that continual love of Jesus for His Father, "My Father!" And He taught His disciples a very simple way of talking to God Himself.

Before Jesus came, God was great in His majesty, great in His creation. And then when Jesus came He became one of us, because His Father loved the world so much that He gave His Son. And Jesus loved His Father and He wanted us to learn to pray by loving one another as the Father has loved Him.

"I love you," He kept on saying, "as the Father loved you, love Him." And His love was the Cross, His love was the bread of life. *Talk Two*

My Words

A prayer, a modified attitude,
A new sympathy, an action?

_____

_____

_____

_____

_____

WEEK FORTY-SEVEN

The Word

Letter of Paul to the Hebrews 12:14

Seek peace with all people, and the holiness without which no one can ever see the Lord.

Living the Word

Mother Teresa arrived in Beirut in August 1982 when the bombing and shelling were at their worst. Ann Petrie related, "Targets were no more than five miles from the Sisters' house. The devastation was horrifying."

Mother Teresa was informed by the Red Cross of the plight of mentally ill and handicapped children whose home, a Muslim charitable center, had been damaged by bombs.

Mother Teresa prayed for a cease-fire so that she could bring them to her Sisters for care. The problem was that the children were located across the Green Line, the no-man's land separating the predominately Muslim sector from East Beirut, home of the Christian Lebanese.

The Sisters joined Mother Teresa in prayer, calling on the Lord for a cease-fire. Ann Petrie and her sister, Jeanette, filmed the drama that followed.

A sudden cease-fire enveloped Beirut; Mother Teresa crossed the Green Line checkpoint into war-ravaged West Beirut, traveling with four Red Cross vehicles. She led in the rescue of thirty-seven youngsters, all suffering from hunger, thirst, and fear. She went among them, embracing them. *SAV 456*

Words of Mother Teresa

I Don't Understand It

"I have never been in a war before," she said in Beirut, "but I have seen famine and death. I was asking myself what do they feel when they do this. I don't understand it. They are all children of God. Why do they do it? I don't understand."

When the expenditure of billions of dollars was justified for what was termed defense, Mother Teresa offered a different meaning for the word. "Today," she asserted, "nations put too much effort and money into defending their borders. If they could only defend defenseless people with food, shelter, and clothing, I think the world would be a happier place."   *SAV 457*

My Words

A prayer, a modified attitude,
A new sympathy, an action?

_____

_____

_____

_____

_____

_____

_____

_____

WEEK FORTY-EIGHT

The Word

Second Letter of Paul to the Corinthians 13:3–5

Since you are asking for a proof that it is Christ who speaks in me; he is not weak with you but his power is at work among you; for, though it was out of weakness that he was crucified, he is alive now with the power of God. We, too, are weak in him, but with regard to you we shall live with him by the power of God.

Living the Word

As she was present to the agony of Calcutta, and that of India's other great cities, so Mother Teresa was present to the anguish of Bhopal, a city four hundred miles south of Delhi, when a cloud of death enveloped a crowded slum on the night of December 3, 1984. The poisoned air, caused by a leak from a pesticide plant, seeped silently into the shantytown, killing many people as they slept. More than twenty-five hundred people died in a few days, and more than one hundred thousand suffered serious injuries to eyes and lungs. The Missionaries of Charity, who had long been working in Bhopal, escaped being among the victims because the death-bringing gas was blown by the wind in a different direction.

Even while the dead were being cremated or buried, Mother Teresa rushed to Bhopal with teams of Missionaries of Charity to work with the Sisters already on the scene. "We have come to love and care for those who most need it in this terrible tragedy," said Mother Teresa, as she went from center to center, from hospital to hospital, visiting the afflicted people. *SAV 468*

Words of Mother Teresa

REDEMPTIVE SUFFERING

Without our suffering, our work would just be social work, very good and helpful, but it would not be the work of Jesus Christ, not part of the Redemption. Jesus wanted to help by sharing our life, our loneliness, our agony, our death. Only by being one with us has He redeemed us. We are allowed to do the same; all the desolation of the poor people, not only their material poverty, but their spiritual destitution, must be redeemed, and we must share it, for only by being one with them can we redeem them, that is, by bringing God into their lives and bringing them to God. *SBFG 67–68*

My Words

A prayer, a modified attitude,
A new sympathy, an action?

_____

_____

_____

_____

_____

_____

_____

_____

_____

WEEK FORTY-NINE

The Word

Second Letter of Paul to the Corinthians 1:3–5

> Blessed be the God and Father of our Lord Jesus Christ, the merciful Father and the God who gives every possible encouragement; he supports us in every hardship, so that we are able to come to the support of others, in every hardship of theirs because of the encouragement that we ourselves receive from God. For just as the sufferings of Christ overflow into our lives; so too does the encouragement we receive through Christ.

Living the Word

There was one small group in Latin America who did not welcome the Sisters and who stunned them by suggesting that it would be better if they left. A certain group of priests told the Sisters that the problems demanded more than they could give. It was time to change the very structures that were giving rise to the poverty with which they were surrounded. The Missionaries of Charity were doing nothing to change these structures, they were told, and were thus prolonging the misery of the people.

The Sisters did not argue but carried on with their own ministry, the backbreaking task of feeding an old woman discharged from a government hospital, washing a rheumy-eyed old drunk left to die on the street, or rescuing little boys and girls abandoned to darkness and hunger.

Mother Teresa said that she was in favor of revolution. She went on to say about herself what had already been said of her, that she was a revolutionary, working for a revolution of love.

SAV 269–70

Words of Mother Teresa

WASTING OUR PRECIOUS LIFE?

There may be times when we appear to be wasting our precious life and burying our talents. Our lives are utterly wasted if we use only the light of reason. Our life has no meaning unless we look at Christ in His poverty.

Today when everything is questioned and changed, let us go back to Nazareth. Jesus had come to redeem the world—to teach us that love of His Father. How strange that He should spend thirty years just doing nothing, wasting His time! Not giving a chance to His personality or to His gifts, for we know that at the age of twelve He silenced the learned priests of the temple, who knew so much and so well. But when His parents found Him, He went down to Nazareth and was subject to them.   *LIS 49*

My Words

> *A prayer, a modified attitude,*
> *A new sympathy, an action?*

_____

_____

_____

_____

_____

_____

_____

WEEK FIFTY

The Word

Letter of Paul to the Colossians 1:3–6

We give thanks for you to God, the Father of our Lord Jesus
Christ, continually in our prayers, ever since we heard about
your faith in Christ Jesus and the love that you show towards
all God's holy people because of the hope which is stored up
for you in heaven. News of this hope reached you not long
ago through the word of truth, the gospel that came to you in
the same way as it is bearing fruit and growing throughout
the world. It has had the same effect among you, ever since
you heard about the grace of God and recognised it for what
it truly is.

Living the Word

When the first soup kitchen was established for the poor on a
very old inner-city street in Madrid, Spain, it was in an area
where there were quite a few bars, mediocre restaurants, and
cheap boardinghouses.

Soon the young disco set became involved and virtually took
over, tearing down walls, removing debris, carrying bricks, and
mixing mortar. As the work progressed, the people who lived
along the street kept wondering what these young people were
doing. They were very curious and sometimes asked, "What are
they trying to do—build their own club or a disco?" But the young
people kept their "secret," until finally the daily presence of
Mother Teresa's Sisters made it clear to all what they were
involved in.   *SOMT 66–67*

Words of Mother Teresa

JOY, A NET OF LOVE

"It is with joy that we must contact Christ under His mask of wretchedness," says Mother Teresa, "because joy is love. Joy is a prayer; joy is strength; joy is a net of love in which you can catch souls. God loves a person who gives joyfully, and the person who gives joyfully gives more. The best way of showing our gratitude to God and to other people is to accept everything joyfully. A joyous heart is the natural result of a heart burning with love."

LWB 63–64

My Words

A prayer, a modified attitude,
A new sympathy, an action?

_____
_____
_____
_____
_____
_____
_____
_____
_____
_____
_____

WEEK FIFTY-ONE

The Word

Second Letter of Paul to the Corinthians 5:17–19

For anyone who is in Christ, there is a new creation: the old order is gone and a new being is there to see. It is all God's work; he reconciled us to himself through Christ and he gave us the ministry of reconciliation. I mean, God was in Christ reconciling the world to himself, not holding anyone's faults against them, but entrusting to us the message of reconciliation.

Living the Word

When the first Global Conference of Spiritual and Parliamentary Leaders on Human Survival was held at Oxford University in April 1988, Mother Teresa was asked to participate. A hundred spiritual, scientific, and political leaders brought their messages. The Dalai Lama warned of damage to the health of planet earth. The scientist Carl Sagan addressed the urgency of using the resources spent on weapons of death for an alternative technology of life for the Third World. Mother Teresa's focus was the human person, image of God, as she had seen that person the preceding night in London's "cardboard city."

"They were inside cardboard boxes like little coffins," she said. "There was one man lying there, protecting himself from cold, with no hope and no home. I shook his hand. He said, 'It is a long time since I felt the warmth of a human hand.' " She brought the message of the needs of the homeless to England's Prime Minister in a personal meeting.   *UNPUB*

Words of Mother Teresa

EVERY ACT OF LOVE A PRAYER

Gandhi said, "He who serves the poor serves God. . . ."
Every act of love is a prayer.

Before we pass this prayer to anyone else, let us put the prayer into life, against death. Prayer in action is love. Love in action is service.   *Talk Three*

"Let us not use bombs and guns to overcome the world. Let us use love and compassion. Let us preach the peace of Christ as He did. He went about doing good. If everyone could see the image of God in his neighbor, do you think we should still need tanks and generals?"   *SAV 479*

My Words

> *A prayer, a modified attitude,*
> *A new sympathy, an action?*

_____

_____

_____

_____

_____

_____

_____

_____

WEEK FIFTY-TWO

The Word

John 15:9–11

> I have loved you
> just as the Father has loved me.
> Remain in my love.
> If you keep my commandments
> you will remain in my love,
> just as I have kept my Father's commandments
> and remain in his love.
> I have told you this
> so that my own joy may be in you
> and your joy be complete.

Living the Word

When little St. Therese died, Mother Teresa related, she was hardly noticed. She had lived so quietly away from the world. When she was declared a saint, the Pope said, "She did ordinary things with extraordinary love." That is what our Sisters are doing around the world: small things, caring for the sick and homeless, washing, cleaning.

Not long ago, in our home for AIDS in New York City, a young man was dying. He was in great pain, but he held on to life hour after hour. The Sister asked him if there was something he needed beside the care he was receiving.

He replied. "I can't die until I ask pardon from my father."

The sister found out where the father was, and he came immediately by plane. The son was reconciled with the father. Then the young man died in love and peace in the Gift of Love home. *Talk Six*

Words of Mother Teresa

We Cannot Give What We Do Not Have

I have one prayer for you. Bring prayer back into the family. Make your family a family of love. Love begins at home.

We cannot give what we do not have. That is why it is necessary to grow in love. And how do we grow in love? By loving, loving until it hurts.

You and I must examine ourselves. Our presence, our voice, what does it give to the people? "Do they look up," as Cardinal Newman's prayer says, "and see only Jesus?"

When we look at the Cross, we know how much Jesus loved us. When we look at the Tabernacle, we know much He loves us now.

We are working in hundreds of houses in eighty countries. Pray for us that we do not spoil God's work. *Talk Six*

My Words

A prayer, a modified attitude,
A new sympathy, an action?

_____

_____

_____

_____

_____

_____

_____

_____

A Retreat in the Spirit of Mother Teresa and the Missionaries of Charity

♦

Sometimes we are drawn to do more praying than is our habit. We might fill this need by following a personal retreat. The word "retreat" is used here in a very general sense. Formal, directed retreats are of a completely different order, as are retreats in a particular setting where spiritual guides are available to retreatants.

We might choose a week of the year, alone or with others, to pray with Mother Teresa and the Missionaries of Charity. Each day starts with a citation from the Constitution prepared by Mother Teresa for the congregation she founded.

The daily prayer recited by the Sisters is followed by the daily litany. Mother Teresa has drawn the prayers and litanies from various sources: "Radiating Christ," for example, comes from Cardinal Newman, while Tuesday's Litany of Humility is attributed to Cardinal Merry del Val. A Co-Worker remarked that before tackling the Litany of Humility, one needs to pray for the courage to recite it.

These prayers are only part of the daily devotional life of the Sisters, whose life is woven with the Eucharist, and who spend an hour daily in the chapel. An hour spent in church for meditation would be fruitful in making this retreat. The retreat could be planned for that stressed week before Christmas, to call to our minds the wondrous mystery of Christ's coming to us in human flesh; it might be timed for Passion Week to conclude with the rising from the tomb of the crucified Messiah. Whenever the week's retreat is planned (even in remembrance of personal or family griefs or joys), the very fact of praying with Mother Teresa and the Missionaries of Charity has special meaning. In union of prayer with them, we can be lifted out of our own concerns, however pressing.

Whether among the lepers of Calcutta, those near death in famine-ridden Africa, the ragpickers of Mexico City, AIDS victims in American cities, or the poorest of the poor in Haiti, the Sisters pray to preserve the same vision. Behind the marred features of the leper, the sunken cheeks and staring eyes of the one near death from starvation, is always hidden the pure glory of God, the blindingly beautiful presence of the Divine—"Christ in a distressing disguise."

We join with the Missionaries of Charity as we search out someone (perhaps someone near to us) who is Christ disguised. It might be a young person who finds the way of Jesus irrelevant and is living a self-destructive life; it might be a lonely old person who needs an ear into which to pour an oft-told (and, yes, boring) tale. Some Co-Workers carry out a work of mercy from their homes, even though family duties may be heavy or illness keeps them housebound. They talk on the telephone with the broken-spirited in their homes and the mentally ill in institutions. They do what they can to lift the hearts of the low in mind and let them know that they are not forgotten. One Co-Worker found that a short telephone call so lifted a man out of his despondency that he said his entire outlook was brightened by the daily call. After a while he suggested that they join in a prayer. His condition so improved that he looked outward to the needs of others. He would pray for the needs of people living out in some way the passion of Christ.

In praying with the Missionaries of Charity, we call on the Sanctifying Spirit to give strength to our often weary hearts and bodies to struggle for better shelter for the homeless in our midst, to serve on a soup line, to witness to the sanctity of life in myriad ways, and to speak for justice. Despite the sorrows, the searing tragedies, and the assaults on human dignity that confront us, we can find joy in awakening in the young, the lonely, the humiliated, or the forsaken the sense of their own infinite dignity as children of the Most High God and brothers and sisters to Jesus.

At the end of the week we can find nourishment in Mother Teresa's meditation, "Who is Jesus to Me?" written in the hospital after Sister Death had come close to her. We can pray to catch her vision of Jesus as our "All in All."

SUNDAY

"Rejoice that once more Christ is walking through the world in you and through you, going about doing good."

M.T.

By feeding daily on the Scriptures, particularly on the New Testament, we shall grow in a deeper and more personal knowledge of Jesus Christ and His teachings, so as to be able to feed His children with the Divine Word. *Const.*

Opening Prayer

Lord Jesus Christ,/ in the depths of Your heart You adore the eternal Father;/ from Him You come as radiant Son,/ begotten in the love of the Holy Spirit./ Bring us close to Your heart that we too,/ sharing Your divine Sonship, may adore the Father who created us in Your likeness./ Heavenly Father, bring all those who do not know You/ to the creative love revealed in the heart of Your Son. Amen.

Radiating Christ

Dear Jesus, help us to spread Your fragrance everywhere we go./ Flood our souls with Your spirit and life./ Penetrate and possess our whole being,/ so utterly,/ that our lives may only be a radiance of Yours./ Shine through us,/ and be so in us,/ that every soul we come in contact with/ may feel Your presence in our soul./ Let them look up and see no longer us/ but only Jesus!/ Stay with us,/ and then we shall begin to shine as You shine;/ so to shine as to be a light to others;/ the light, O Jesus, will be all from You,/ none of it will be ours;/ it will be You, shining on others through us./ Let us thus praise You in the way You love best/ by shining on those around us./ Let us preach You without preaching,/ not by words but by our example,/ by the catching force,/ the sympathetic influence of what we do,/ the evident fullness of the love our hearts bear/ to You. Amen.

Litany of the Holy Name of Jesus

Lord, have mercy on us.

Christ, have mercy on us.

Lord, have mercy on us.

Jesus, hear us.

Jesus, graciously hear us.

God, the Father of Heaven,
   HAVE MERCY ON US.

God, the Son, Redeemer of the world,

God, the Holy Spirit,

Holy Trinity, one God,

Jesus, Son of the living God,

Jesus, splendor of the Father,

Jesus, brightness of eternal light,

Jesus, King of glory,

Jesus, Son of justice,

Jesus, Son of the Virgin Mary,

Jesus, most amiable,

Jesus, most admirable,

Jesus, mighty God,

Jesus, father of the world to come,

Jesus, angel of great counsel,

Jesus, most powerful,

Jesus, most patient,

Jesus, most obedient,

Jesus, meek and humble of heart,

Jesus, lover of chastity,

Jesus, lover of us,

Jesus, the God of peace,

Jesus, the Author of life,

Jesus, example of virtues,

Jesus, zealous lover of souls,

Jesus, our God,

Jesus, our refuge,

Jesus, the Father of the poor,

Jesus, treasure of the faithful,

Jesus, the Good Shepherd,

Jesus, the true light,

Jesus, eternal wisdom,

Jesus, infinite goodness,

Jesus, our way and our life,

Jesus, the joy of angels,

Jesus, the King of Patriarchs,

Jesus, the master of the Apostles,

Jesus, the teacher of the Evangelists,

Jesus, the strength of martyrs,

Jesus, the light of confessors,

Jesus, the purity of virgins,

Jesus, the crown of all Saints,

Be merciful unto us.

Jesus, spare us.

Be merciful unto us.

Jesus, hear us.

From all evil,

   JESUS DELIVER US.

From all sin,

From your wrath,

From the snares of the devil,

From the spirit of uncleanness,

From everlasting death,

From the neglect of Your inspirations,

Through the mystery of Your holy Incarnation,

Through Your nativity,

Through Your infancy,

Through Your most divine life,

Through Your labors,

Through Your agony and passion,

Through Your Cross and dereliction,

Through Your faintness and weariness,

Through Your death and burial,

Through Your Resurrection,

Through Your Ascension,

Through Your institution of the most Holy
Eucharist,

Through Your joys,

Through Your glory,

Lamb of God, You take away the sins of the
world, spare us, O Jesus.

Lamb of God, You take away the sins of the
world, graciously hear us, O Jesus.

Lamb of God, You take away the sins of the
world, have mercy on us, O Jesus,

Jesus, hear us.

Jesus, graciously hear us.

Let us pray

O Lord Jesus Christ, who said: Ask and you shall receive, seek and
you shall find, knock and it shall be opened unto you, grant we
beseech You to us Your supplicants, the gift of Your most divine
love, that we may love You with our whole hearts and in all our
words and works, and never cease from praising You.

O Lord, give us a perpetual fear as well as love of Your Holy
Name, for You never cease to govern those You founded upon the
solidity of Your love, Who live and reign world without end.
Amen.

MONDAY

"If there are poor on the moon, we will go there too."

M.T.

The spiritual and apostolic fruitfulness of our Society will depend on:

- our deliberate choice of simple and lowly means in the fulfillment of our mission;
- our joyful fidelity to the humble works among the poorest of the poor that comes from living the utter lowliness and self-effacement of Christ, which leads us to identify ourselves with the poor we serve,
- sharing their poverty and their fate until it hurts; our complete dependence on God's Providence for all our needs. *Const.*

Opening Prayer

We praise and adore You, Divine Providence.
We resign ourselves entirely to all Your just and holy designs.

Let us pray

Eternal God,/ Your eyes are upon all Your works,/ especially intent on Your servants,/ turn away from us whatever is hurtful and grant us whatever is advantageous,/ that through Your favor/ and under the benign influence of Your special Providence/ we may securely pass through the transitory dangers and difficulties of this life/ and happily arrive at the eternal joys of the next. Through Christ Our Lord. Amen.

Prayer Before Leaving for Work

Dear Lord, the Great Healer, I kneel before You, since every perfect gift must come from You. I pray, give skill to my hands, clear vision to my mind, kindness and meekness to my heart. Give me singleness of purpose, strength to lift up a part of the burden of my suffering fellowmen, and a true realization of the privilege that is mine. Take from my heart all guile and worldliness that with the simple faith of a child, I may rely on You. Amen.

Litany of the Holy Spirit

Lord, have mercy on us.
Christ, have mercy on us.
Lord, have mercy on us.
Christ, hear us.
Christ, graciously hear us.
God, the Father of heaven,
   HAVE MERCY ON US.

God, the Son, Redeemer of the world,
God, the Holy Spirit,
Holy Spirit, who proceeds from the Father and
   the Son,
Holy Spirit, coequal with the Father and
   the Son,
Promise of the Father, most loving and most
   bounteous,
Gift of the Most High God,
Ray of heavenly light,
Author of all good,
Source of living water,
Consuming fire,
Burning love,

Spiritual unction,

Spirit of truth and power,

Spirit of wisdom and understanding,

Spirit of counsel and fortitude,

Spirit of knowledge and piety,

Spirit of the fear of the Lord.

Spirit of compunction and penance,

Spirit of grace and of prayer,

Spirit of charity, peace, and joy,

Spirit of patience, longanimity, and goodness,

Spirit of benignity, continence, and chastity,

Spirit of the adoption of the sons of God,

Holy Spirit, the Comforter,

Holy Spirit, the Sanctifier

Who in the beginning moved over
    the waters,

By whose inspiration spoke the holy men
    of God,

Who did cooperate in the miraculous conception
    of the Son of God,

Who did descend upon Him at His Baptism,

Who on the day of Pentecost did appear in
    fiery tongues upon the disciples
    of our Lord,

By whom we also are born,

Who dwells in us,

Who governs the Church,

Who fills the whole world,

Holy Spirit, hear us.

That You write Your law in our hearts,
    WE BESEECH YOU HEAR US.

That You shed abroad Your light in our hearts,

That You inflame us with the fire of Your love,

That You open to us the treasures of Your
    grace,

That You teach us to ask for them according
  to Your Will,
That You enlighten us with Your heavenly
  inspirations,
That You lead us in the way of Your
  commandments,
That You keep us to Yourself by Your
  powerful attractions,
That You grant us the knowledge that alone
  is necessary,
That You make us obedient to Your
  inspirations,

That You teach us to pray, and Yourself
  pray with us.
That You clothe us with love toward our
  brethren,
That You inspire us with horror of evil,
That You direct us in the practice of good,
That You give us the grace of all virtues,
That You cause us to persevere in justice,
That You be Yourself our everlasting reward,
Lamb of God, who takes away the sins of the
  world, spare us, O Lord.
Lamb of God, who takes away the sins of the
  world, graciously hear us, O Lord.
Lamb of God, who takes away the sins of the
  world, have mercy on us, O Lord.
Holy Spirit, hear us.
Holy Spirit, graciously hear us.
Lord, have mercy on us.
Christ, have mercy on us.
Create in us a clean heart, O God,
And renew a right spirit in us.

Let us pray

Grant, O Merciful Father, that Your divine Spirit may enlighten, inflame, and cleanse our hearts, that He may penetrate us with His heavenly dew and make us fruitful in good works, through Jesus Christ, Our Lord. Amen.

TUESDAY

"Let Us Make Our Society Something Beautiful for God."

M.T.

As Missionaries of Charity we must be:

- carriers of God's love, ready to go in haste like Mary in search of souls; . . .

- souls consumed with one desire, Jesus, keeping His interests continually in our hearts and minds, carrying Our Lord to places where He has not walked before:

- fearless in doing the things He did and courageously go through danger and death with Him and for Him; . . .

- ever ready to go to any part of the world at any time, to respect and appreciate unfamiliar customs of other peoples, their living conditions and language, willing to adapt ourselves if and when necessary.   *Const.*

Opening Prayer

Holy Angels, our advocates,
Holy Angels, our brothers,
Holy Angels, our counselors,
Holy Angels, our defenders,
Holy Angels, our enlighteners,
Holy Angels, our friends,
Holy Angels, our guides,
Holy Angels, our helpers,
Holy Angels, our intercessors,
Lamb of God, etc. *(3 times)*

Pray
for
us

O Holy Angels,/ guardians of the poor confided to our care,/ we entreat your intercession for them and for ourselves./ Obtain of God to crown His work by giving a blessing to our endeavors,/ that so we may promote His greater honor and glory procuring their salvation./ Through Christ Our Lord. Amen.

Litany of Humility

Lord, have mercy on us.
Christ, have mercy on us.
Lord, have mercy on us.
Christ, hear us.
Christ, graciously hear us.
God, the Father of Heaven,
    HAVE MERCY ON US.
God, the Son, Redeemer of the world,
God, the Holy Spirit,
Holy Trinity, One God,
O Jesus, meek and humble of heart,
Make our hearts like Yours.
From the desire of being esteemed,
    DELIVER ME, O JESUS.
From the desire of being loved,
From the desire of being extolled,
From the desire of being honored,
From the desire of being praised,
From the desire of being preferred,
From the desire of being consulted,
From the desire of being approved,
From the desire of being popular,
From the fear of being humiliated,
From the fear of being despised,
From the fear of suffering rebukes,
From the fear of being calumniated,

From the fear of being forgotten,
From the fear of being wronged,
From the fear of being ridiculed,
From the fear of being suspected,
That others may be loved more than I,
JESUS, GRANT ME THE GRACE
    TO DESIRE IT
That others may be esteemed more than I,
That in the opinion of the world, others may
    increase and I may decrease,
That others may be chosen and I set aside,
That others may be praised and I unnoticed,
That others may be preferred to me in
    everything,
That others may become holier than I,
    provided that I may become as holy as
    I should,

Lamb of God, who takes away the sins of the
    world, spare us. O Lord.
Lamb of God, who takes away the sins of
    the world, graciously hear us, O Lord.
Lamb of God, who takes away the sins of the
    world, have mercy on us, O Lord.

Let us pray

O Lord Jesus Christ, who said: Ask and you shall receive, seek and you shall find, knock and it shall be opened unto you, grant, we beseech You, to us Your supplicants, the gift of Your most divine love, that we may love You with our whole hearts and in all our words and works, and never cease from praising You.

O Lord, give us a perpetual fear as well as love of Your Holy Name, for You never cease to govern those You founded upon the solidity of Your love, who live and reign world without end, Amen.

WEDNESDAY

Christ's call to give WHOLEHEARTED and Free Service to the poorest of the poor. WHOLEHEARTED means:

- with hearts burning with zeal and love for souls;
- with single-minded devotion, wholly rooted in our deep union with God in prayer and fraternal love;
- that we give them not only our hands to serve, but our hearts to love with kindness and humility;
- entirely at the disposal of the poor;
- hard labor without counting the cost.   *Const*

Opening Prayer

O Glorious St. Joseph,/ we most humbly beg of you, by the love and care you had for Jesus and Mary,/ to take our affairs, spiritual and temporal, into your hands./ Direct them to the greater glory of God,/ and obtain for us the grace to do His holy Will. Amen.

Prayer for Peace

Lord, make me a channel of your peace, that
where there is hatred,
    I may bring love;
where there is wrong,
    I may bring the spirit of forgiveness;
where there is discord,
    I may bring harmony;

where there is error,
    I may bring truth;
where there is doubt,
    I may bring faith;
where there is despair,
    I may bring hope;
where there are shadows,
    I may bring light;
where there is sadness,
    I may bring joy;
Lord, grant that I may seek rather
    to comfort than to be comforted;
to understand than to be understood;
to love than to be loved;
for it is by forgetting self that one finds,
it is by forgiving that one is forgiven,
it is by dying that one awakens to eternal life.
                                Amen.

Litany of St. Joseph

Lord, have mercy on us.
Christ, have mercy on us.
Lord, have mercy on us.
Christ, hear us.
Christ, graciously hear us.
God the Father of Heaven,
    HAVE MERCY ON US.
God the Son, Redeemer of the world,
God the Holy Spirit.
Holy Trinity One God,
Holy Mary,
PRAY FOR US.
Saint Joseph,
Illustrious Scion of David,

Light of Patriarchs,
Spouse of the Mother of God,
Chaste guardian of the Virgin,
Foster father of the Son of God,
Diligent defender of Christ,
Head of the Holy Family,
Joseph most just,
Joseph most chaste,
Joseph most prudent,
Joseph most obedient,
Joseph most faithful,
Mirror of patience,
Lover of poverty,
Model of workers,
Ornament of domestic life,
Guardian of virgins,
Safeguard of families,
Consolation of the poor,
Hope of the sick,
Patron of the dying,
Terror of demons,
Protector of Holy Church,

Lamb of God, who takes away the sins of
    the world, spare us, O Lord.
Lamb of God, who takes away the sins of
    the world, graciously hear us, O Lord.
Lamb of God, who takes away the sins of
    the world, have mercy on us.
He has placed him Lord of His house.
And prince of all His possessions.

Let us pray

O God, who by an ineffable providence was pleased to elect the Blessed Joseph as spouse of Thy Mother, grant, we beseech Thee, that as we venerate him as protector on earth, we may deserve to have him as intercessor in heaven, who lives and reigns world without end. Amen.

THURSDAY

Christ's call to give Wholehearted and FREE Service to the poorest of the poor. FREE means:

- joyfully and with eagerness;
- fearlessly and openly;
- freely giving what we have freely received;
- without accepting any return in cash or in kind;
- without seeking any reward or gratitude. *Const.*

Opening Prayer

Lord Jesus,/ Our God and Savior,/ we believe that You are present in this sacrament of Your Love,/ a memorial of Your death and resurrection,/ a sign of unity and a bond of charity./ In Your humanity, You veiled Your glory, You disappear still more in the Eucharist,/ to be broken,/ to become the food of men./ Lord Jesus,/ give us the faith and strength to die to ourselves/ in order to become a harvest for You,/ so that You may continue through us/ to give life to men./ May our minds be ever filled with You,/ the pledge of our future glory. Amen.

The Taize Prayer

O God, the Father of all,
You ask every one of us to spread
Love where the poor are humiliated,
Joy where the Church is brought low,

And reconciliation where people are
    divided—
  Father against son,
  Mother against daughter,
  Husband against wife,
  Believers against those who cannot
    believe,
  Christians against their unloved fellow
    Christians.
You open the way for us, so that the
  wounded body of
Jesus Christ, Your Church, may be leaven
  of Communion,
for the poor of the earth and in the
  whole human family.

*Prayer composed by Mother Teresa and
  Brother Roger.*

Litany of the Sacred Heart

  Lord, have mercy on us.
  Christ, have mercy on us.
  Lord, have mercy on us.
  Christ, hear us.
  Christ, graciously hear us.
  God, the Father of Heaven,
    HAVE MERCY ON US.
  God, the Son, Redeemer of the world,
  God, the Holy Spirit,
  Holy Trinity, One God,
  Heart of Jesus, Son of the eternal Father,
  Heart of Jesus, formed by the Holy Spirit in
    the Virgin Mother's womb,
  Heart of Jesus, substantially united to the
    word of God,

Heart of Jesus of infinite majesty,

Heart of Jesus, Holy Temple of God,

Heart of Jesus, tabernacle of the Most High

Heart of Jesus, house of God and gate of
heaven,

Heart of Jesus, glowing furnace of charity,

Heart of Jesus, vessel of justice and love,

Heart of Jesus, full of goodness and mercy,

Heart of Jesus, abyss of all virtues,

Heart of Jesus, most worthy of all Praise.

Heart of Jesus, king and center of all hearts,

Heart of Jesus, containing all the treasures
of wisdom and knowledge,

Heart of Jesus, having all the fullness of
the Godhead,

Heart of Jesus in whom the Father is well
pleased,

Heart of Jesus, of whose fullness we have
received,

Heart of Jesus, desire of the everlasting hills,

Heart of Jesus, patient and rich in mercy,

Heart of Jesus, enriching all who call upon
Thee,

Heart of Jesus, fount of life and holiness,

Heart of Jesus, propitiation of our offenses,

Heart of Jesus, overwhelmed with reproaches,

Heart of Jesus, bruised for our iniquities,

Heart of Jesus, obedient even unto death,

Heart of Jesus, pierced with a lance,

Heart of Jesus, source of all consolation,

Heart of Jesus, our life and resurrection,

Heart of Jesus, our peace and reconciliation,

Heart of Jesus, victim for our sins,

Heart of Jesus, salvation of those who hope in
You,

Heart of Jesus, hope of those who die in You,

Heart of Jesus, delight of all saints,

Lamb of God, who takes away the sins of
the world, spare us, O Lord,
Lamb of God, who takes away the sins of
the world, graciously hear us, O Lord,
Lamb of God, who takes away the sins of
the world, have mercy on us.

Let us pray

Almighty and everlasting God, look on the Heart of Your Son and
the praise and satisfaction He offers You for sinners. In Your
goodness, pardon those who ask Your mercy in the name of Your
Son, Jesus Christ, who lives and reigns with You forever and ever.
Amen.

FRIDAY

Christ's call to give Wholehearted and Free SERVICE to the poorest of the poor. SERVICE means:

- an unceasing and wholehearted labor in making ourselves available to Jesus so that He may live, in and through us, His life of infinitely tender, compassionate, and merciful love for the spiritually and materially poorest of the poor. We need to be pure of heart to see Jesus in the person of the poorest of the poor. Therefore, the more repugnant the work, or the more disfigured or deformed the image of God in the person, the greater will be our faith and loving devotion in seeking the face of Jesus and lovingly ministering to Him in the distressing disguise. *Const.*

Opening Prayer

O Sacred Heart of Jesus, humbly prostrate before You,/ we come to renew our consecration,/ with the resolution of repairing,/ by an increase of love and fidelity to You,/ all the outrages unceasingly offered You./ We firmly purpose:

The more Your mysteries are blasphemed, the more firmly we shall believe them,/ O Sacred Heart of Jesus!

The more impiety endeavors to extinguish our hopes of immortality,
the more we shall trust in Your Heart,/ sole hope of mortals!/

The more hearts resist Your divine attractions,
the more we shall love You,/ O infinitely amiable Heart of Jesus!

The more Your divinity is attacked, the more we shall adore it,/ O divine Heart of Jesus!

The more Your holy laws are forgotten and transgressed, the more we shall observe them,/ O most/ holy Heart of Jesus!

The more Your sacraments are despised and abandoned, the more we shall receive them with love and respect,/ O most liberal Heart of Jesus!

The more Your adorable virtues are forgotten, the more we shall endeavor to practice them,/ O Heart, model of every virtue!

The more the demon labors to destroy souls, the more we shall be inflamed with a desire to save them,/ O Heart of Jesus, zealous lover of souls!

The more pride and sensuality tend to destroy abnegation and love of duty, the more generous we shall be in overcoming ourselves,/ O Heart of Jesus!

O Sacred Heart,/ give us so strong and powerful a grace that we may be Your apostles in the midst of the world,/ and Your crown in a happy eternity. Amen.

Anima Christi

Soul of Christ, sanctify me,
Body of Christ, save me,
Blood of Christ, inebriate me,
Water from the side of Christ, wash me,
Passion of Christ, strengthen me,
O Good Jesus, hear me,
Within Thy wounds hide me,
Suffer me not to be separated from Thee,
From the malicious enemy defend me,
In the hour of my death call me,
And bid me come unto Thee,
That with Thy Saints I may praise Thee.
Forever and ever. Amen.

Litany of the Passion of Our Lord

Lord, have mercy on us.
Christ, have mercy on us.
Lord, have mercy on us.
Christ, hear us.
Christ, graciously hear us
God, the Father of heaven,
    HAVE MERCY ON US.
God, the Son, Redeemer of the world,
God, the Holy Spirit,
Holy Trinity, one God,

Jesus Christ, who for our redemption came
    down from heaven,
    HAVE MERCY ON US.
Jesus Christ, who was born of the glorious
    Virgin Mary,
Jesus Christ, who for us took the form of a
    servant,
Jesus Christ, who lay in the manger,
Jesus Christ, who did not disdain to weep as
    a sinner,
Jesus Christ, who macerated Your body with
    hunger and thirst,
Jesus Christ, who for us continued in prayer,
    even unto a bloody sweat;
Jesus Christ, who suffered Yourself to be
    betrayed with a kiss by Judas,
Jesus Christ, who was taken and cast down
    upon the ground,
Jesus Christ, who suffered Yourself to be led
    with Your hands bound behind Your back,

Jesus Christ, who was brought before the chief
    priests and falsely accused,

Jesus Christ, who was smitten on the face
  with blows and stripes,

Jesus Christ, who was mocked with diverse
  reproaches,

Jesus Christ, who was delivered to Pilate,

Jesus Christ, who was tied to the pillar and
  scourged, even unto blood,

Jesus Christ, who was clothed with a purple
  garment by the soldiers,

Jesus Christ, who was crowned with hard and
  sharp thorns,

Jesus Christ, who so often heard those most
  cruel words: Away with Him, crucify Him,

Jesus Christ, who being wearied and burdened,
  bore the hard wood of the Cross,

Jesus Christ, who being lifted up on the Cross,
  was made the companion of thieves,

Jesus Christ, who having Your hands and
  feet nailed to the Cross, was blasphemed
  by those who passed by,

Jesus Christ, whose beautiful face was made
  as it were leprous,

Jesus Christ, who prayed to Your Father for
  those that crucified You, and graciously
  heard the thief upon the Cross,

Jesus Christ, who recommended Your
  most dear Mother to St. John,

Jesus Christ, who was pierced with a spear
and redeemed the world with Your own Blood,

Jesus Christ, who was laid in a sepulchre,

Jesus Christ, who rose from the dead the third
  day,

Jesus Christ, who forty days afterward
  ascended into heaven,

Jesus Christ, who sits at the right hand of the
  Father,

Jesus Christ, who will come to judge the living
    and the dead,

Lamb of God, You take away the sins of the
    world, spare us, O Lord.
Lamb of God, You take away the sins of
    the world, graciously hear us, O Lord.
Lamb of God, You take away the sins of
    the world, have mercy on us, O Lord.
Christ, hear us.
Christ, graciously hear us.
Lord, have mercy on us.
Christ, have mercy on us.
Lord, have mercy on us.
Our Father. . . .

Let Us Pray

We beseech you, O Lord Jesus Christ, that the Blessed Virgin
Mary may intercede for us with Your clemency, both now and at
the hour of our death, who at the hour of Your Passion had her
most holy soul pierced through with the sword of sorrow. Amen.

SATURDAY

SERVICE also means: immediate and effective service to the poorest of the poor as long as they have no one to help them by: feeding the hungry

- not only with food, but also with the Word of God; giving drink to the thirsty
- not only for water, but for knowledge, peace, truth, justice, and love; clothing the naked
- not only with clothes, but also with human dignity; giving shelter to the homeless
- not only a shelter made with bricks, but a heart that understands, that covers, that loves; nursing the sick and dying
- not only of the body, but also of the mind and spirit.

Const.

Opening Prayer

O Heart of Mary,/ Heart of the tenderest of Mothers,/ Cause of our Joy,/ we consecrate ourselves unreservedly to you,/ our hearts, our bodies, our souls;/ we desire to belong to you, in life and in death./ You know, O Immaculate Mother, that your Divine Son has chosen us in His infinite Mercy/ in spite of our misery and sinfulness,/ not only as His children and His spouses/ but also as His victims,/ to console His Divine Heart in the Sacrament of His love,/ to atone for sacrileges,/ and to obtain pardon for poor sinners./ We come today to offer Him through your most Pure Heart,/ the entire sacrifice of ourselves./ Of our own free choice we renounce all the desires and inclinations of our corrupt nature,/ and we accept willingly and lovingly whatever sufferings He may be pleased to send us./ But conscious of our weakness,/ we implore you,/ O holy Mother, to shield us with your maternal protection/ and to obtain from your Divine Son all the graces we need to persevere./ Bless our society, this house, and the houses we visit,/ and each soul confided to our care,/ our relations, friends, benefactors that all may persevere in grace or recover it if lost, and when the hour of death comes,/ may our hearts, modeled on your Immaculate Heart,/ breathe forth their last sigh into the Heart of Your Divine Son./ Amen.

Prayer of Pope Paul VI

Make us worthy, Lord,/ to serve our fellow-men throughout the world/ who live and die in poverty and hunger./ Give them through our hands, this day their daily bread,/ and by our understanding love, give peace and joy./

Litany of Our Lady

Lord, have mercy on us.
Christ, have mercy on us.
Lord, have mercy on us.
Christ, hear us.
Christ, graciously hear us.
God, the Father of Heaven,
    HAVE MERCY ON US.
God, the Son, Redeemer of the world,
God, the Holy Spirit,
Holy Trinity, One God,

Holy Mary,
    PRAY FOR US.
Holy Mother of God,
Holy Virgin of Virgins,

Mother of Christ;
Mother of divine grace,
Mother most pure,
Mother most chaste,
Mother inviolate;
Mother undefiled,
Mother most amiable,
Mother most admirable,
Mother of good counsel,
Mother of our Creator,

Mother of our Savior,
Virgin most prudent,
Virgin most venerable,
Virgin most renowned,
Virgin most powerful,
Virgin most merciful,
Virgin most faithful,
Mirror of justice,
Seat of wisdom,
Cause of our joy,
Spiritual vessel,
Vessel of honor,
Vessel of singular devotion,
Mystical rose,
Tower of David,
Tower of ivory,
House of gold,
Ark of the Covenant,
Gate of Heaven,
Morning star,
Health of the sick,
Refuge of sinners,
Comforter of the afflicted,
Help of Christians,
Queen of Angels,
Queen of patriarchs,

Queen of prophets,
Queen of apostles,
Queen of martyrs,
Queen of confessors,
Queen of virgins,
Queen of all saints,
Queen conceived without original sin,
Queen of the most Holy Rosary,
Queen assumed into Heaven,
Queen of Peace,

Lamb of God, who takes away the sins of the
world, spare us, O Lord
Lamb of God, who takes away the sins of the
world, graciously hear us. O Lord
Lamb of God, who takes away the sins of the
world, have mercy on us,
Pray for us, O Holy Mother of God.
That we may be made worthy of the
promises of Christ.

Let Us Pray

Pour forth, We beseech You, O Lord, Your grace into our hearts,
that we, to whom the Incarnation of Christ Your Son was made
known by the message of an angel, may by His Passion and Cross
be brought to the glory of His resurrection through the same
Christ Our Lord. Amen.

END-OF-RETREAT MEDITATION

Who Is Jesus to Me?

This is Jesus to me:
The Word made flesh.
The Bread of life.
The Victim offered for our sins on the Cross.
The Sacrifice offered at the Holy Mass for the sins of
    the world and mine.
The Word—to be spoken.
The Truth—to be told.
The Way—to be walked.
The Light—to be lit.
The Life—to be lived.
The Love—to be loved.
The Joy—to be shared.
The Sacrifice—to be offered.
The Peace—to be given.
The Bread of Life—to be eaten.
The Hungry—to be fed.
The Thirsty—to be satiated.
The Naked—to be clothed.
The Homeless—to be taken in.
The Sick—to be healed.
The Lonely—to be loved.
The Unwanted—to be wanted.
The Leper—to wash his wounds.
The Beggar—to give him a smile.
The Drunkard—to listen to him.
The Retarded—to protect him.
The Little One—to embrace him.
The Blind—to lead him.

The Dumb—to speak for him.
The Crippled—to walk with him.
The Drug Addict—to befriend him.
The Prostitute—to remove from danger and befriend her.
The Prisoner—to be visited.
The Old—to be served.

To me Jesus is my God.
        Jesus is my Spouse.
        Jesus is my Life.
        Jesus is my only Love.
        Jesus is my All in All.
        Jesus is my Everything.

Sources

◆

Talk One   Nobel Award Speech, December 10, 1979

Talk Two   Berlin, June 8, 1981 (excerpts SAV 495)

Talk Three   St. James Church, London, July 7, 1981

Talk Four   Co-Workers Meeting, St. Paul, Minnesota, June 1986

Talk Five   United Nations General Assembly Hall, New York, New York, October 16, 1986, at premiere of Petrie Production documentary *Mother Teresa* (excerpt SAV 491-92)

Talk Six   International Co-Workers Meeting, Paris, May 12, 1988

CoW-N   Co-Workers Newsletter, Co-Workers of Mother Teresa in America (published twice per year)

Const.   Constitutions of the Missionaries of Charity, Calcutta, 1988

Unpub.   Unpublished

GFG   Mother Teresa of Calcutta: *A Gift for God, Prayers and Meditations.* San Francisco: Harper and Row, 1975

LIS   Spink, Kathryn, ed. Mother Teresa: *Life in the Spirit, Reflections, Meditations and Prayers.* San Francisco: Harper and Row, 1983

LWB   Gorree, Georges, and Jean Barbier. *Love Without Boundaries.* Huntington, Indiana: Our Sunday Visitor, 1974

MBMS   Mosteller, Sister Sue. *My Brother, My Sister.* New York: Paulist Press, 1972

MDV   Collins, Alice. *My Daily Visitor.* Huntington, Indiana: Our Sunday Visitor, 1978

MLFP   Balado-Gonzalez, José Luis, and Janet N. Playfoot, eds. *My Life for the Poor*. San Francisco: Harper and Row, 1985

SAV   Egan, Eileen. *Such A Vision of the Street, Mother Teresa—The Spirit and the Work*. New York: Doubleday—Image Books, 1986

SBFG   Muggeridge, Malcolm. *Something Beautiful for God*. New York: Harper and Row, 1971

SOMT   Balado-Gonzalez, José Luis. *Stories of Mother Teresa—Her Smile and Her Words*. Liguori, Missouri: Liguori Publications, 1983

TGLC   McGovern, James. *To Give the Love of Christ*. New York: Emmaus Books, Paulist Press, 1978

WDI   Le Joly, Edward, S.J. *We Do It for Jesus—Mother Teresa and Her Missionaries*. London: Darton, Longman and Todd, 1977

WTLB   Mother Teresa. *Words to Love By*. Notre Dame, Indiana: Ave Maria Press, 1983

All scriptural quotations are taken from *The New Jerusalem Bible*, Garden City, N.Y.: Doubleday, 1985.

CO-WORKERS OF MOTHER TERESA
NATIONAL LINKS—U.S.A.

Ed and Dorothy Baroch
2026 Crestmont Drive
Moses Lake
Washington 98837
U.S.A.

My Words

◆